A Good Day's Work

Putting up hay.

A Good Day's Work

An Iowa Farm in the Great Depression

Dwight W. Hoover

Ivan R. Dee   Chicago   2007

www.ivanrdee.com

Photo credits: frontispiece and pages 2, 11, 53, 99, 157, 176, A. M. Wettach Collection, State Historical Society of Iowa; pages 38, 78, 124, Hoover family photographs.

Library of Congress Cataloging-in-Publication Data:
Hoover, Dwight W., 1926–
    A good day's work : an Iowa farm in the Great Depression / Dwight W. Hoover.
        p. cm.
    Includes index.
    ISBN-13: 978-1-56663-702-2 (cloth : alk. paper)
    ISBN-10: 1-56663-702-3 (cloth : alk. paper)
1. Hoover, Dwight W., 1926—Childhood and youth. 2. Hoover, Dwight W., 1926—Family. 3. Farm life—Iowa—Mahaska County—History—20th century. 4. Seasons—Iowa—Mahaska County. 5. Mahaska County (Iowa)—Social life and customs—20th century. 6. Mahaska County (Iowa)—Biography. 7. Depressions—1929—Iowa—Mahaska County. 8. Agriculture—Iowa—Mahaska County—History—20th century. I. Title. F627.M2H75 2006
    977.7'84033092—dc22
    [B]
                                                                2006037084

To Adrian Dwight Hoffer and Owen George Hoffer,
my grandsons, whose amazing energy and immense curiosity
would have made them great farmers

Acknowledgments

WHEN I BEGAN this project at the suggestion of my editor, Ivan Dee, I had two misconceptions. One was that it would be largely an individual task, the other that it would be difficult to recall events of more than sixty years ago. Both ideas were wrong.

My wife, Jan Holmes, became involved from the start and contributed many ideas as well as the computer skills that made the book possible. She prodded me to consult others for additional insights and for comments on earlier drafts. The list of helpers expanded as time went on.

My sisters, Alice and Helen, added to the book and provided a different view of our early lives. Two of my cousins, Dale and Lyle, read the manuscript and, I fear, praised my efforts more than they deserved. Dale, who spent his career as an agricultural economist, in particular added professional suggestions. I was struck in reading both their appraisals how much our differences in age (both are younger than I) altered our experiences.

Bill and Penny Cupp, friends and former Iowans, added their knowledge as writers and editors. Roy Hampton, one of a number of friends and native Iowans living in a retirement center in Indianola, helped immensely by telling me about the images in the A. M. Wettach Collection at the State Historical Society of Iowa. Wilmer Tjossem organized others to comment on the manuscript; among them was Robert A. Rohwer, who retired after a life of farming. He corrected many of my errors, added details I had forgotten, and in general made this a much better book. Mary Kummings helped by exploring FFA archives in Indianapolis.

Two individuals at the State Historical Society of Iowa went out of their way to help my wife and me locate the photographs credited in this book. Mary Bennett and Charles Scott were generous with their time and ideas and made our efforts much easier.

Finally, Ivan Dee was deeply involved in the development of this book from conception to organization to editing. His support made my task much easier and this book much better.

With the help of these individuals the writing of the book became more pleasant. Their insights reminded me of times and events that remained hazy in my mind and saved me from making unintended mistakes. Any remaining are mine alone.

D. W. H.

Sarasota, Florida
February 2007

Contents

A Good Day's Work

Alone.

Sunup: A Nineteenth-Century Farm

☙ I WAS BORN on my father's farm in Harrison Township, Mahaska County, Iowa, in 1926. Sometimes I cannot distinguish between my own memories of an event and a version told to me. My recollections of my preschool days are vague and cloudy; I can only say with certainty that I remember being ill with pneumonia when I was four, because I recall having to learn to walk all over again. I even remember feeling spaced out the day before I became sick, a feeling I have never had since but would not mind having again.

In recalling my early years, I thought the farm would be a record and a physical reminder of the past, one that would serve as a tangible marker, an unchanging truth. But I was mistaken.

Now I realize that the farm was really a nineteenth-century operation in the process of changing, being transformed into something quite different. I grew up in a unique time that can be recaptured only in old photographs and in the memories of those who lived in that age. It was, in a sense, a premodern era, one that would not be unfamiliar to a boy who lived in the 1890s. The farm was a capitalistic enterprise overlaid on a subsistence occupation, a family farm that provided its residents with most of their food but also with crops that brought needed cash in a market economy.

My ancestors came to Pennsylvania in the 1730s from the Palatinate in southwest Germany. Their name was originally Huber, changed to Hoover in the New World; they were Pietists who became Quakers. Migrating down the Shenandoah Valley to North Carolina, they moved again following the War of 1812 and the subsequent opening of land in the eastern Midwest—Ohio, Indiana, and Illinois—as the Native Americans were replaced in the 1820s and 1830s. Their motives were both ideological and economic: they opposed slavery, which was expanding in the South, and they wanted the fertile land of the eastern prairie.

The particular branch of Hoovers from which I descended went even farther west. They moved to Iowa Territory before it became a state in 1845, without stopping in Ohio for a time as did President Herbert Hoover's family. Our family, under the leadership of Jonas Hoover, my great great-grandfather, settled in an area to farm near what was to become the town of Oskaloosa in Mahaska County.

The land these early settlers sought had to have certain characteristics: a nearby water source, a supply of wood for building both houses and barns, and good fertile land. These could be found in abundance but not necessarily together. And these qualities did not make for the best farms for every purpose. Trees to furnish wood, such as white oak, grew on soil that was less fertile than open prairie, and the land nearest the streams was more rolling and more susceptible to erosion. But the pioneers distrusted land that was too flat since it might be marshy and slow to drain before tilling.

The original Hoover homestead was on land typically settled by the early pioneers, a little hilly but close to the water of Spring Creek, wooded but with good arable land.

Although the first Hoover farms were primarily for subsistence, by the time my grandfather was born in 1865 a cash crop had appeared. It was not grain but wool.

My great-grandfather began the Hoover identification with sheep, though he sometimes grew unhappy with them. According to family lore, he once tired of raising sheep and sold them all. A week later he purchased another large flock. When asked why, he replied that he could not sleep because he missed the sound of sheep's bells.

As was common at the time, he had a large family that eventually spread out in the immediate neighborhood into their own small farms. In the days of horse-drawn equipment, most believed the maximum amount of land that one man could cultivate by himself was 80 acres. If some of the land were used for pasture, wood lots, and such, the farm might be larger, perhaps even covering a quarter-section (160 acres).

My own grandfather tilled a 120-acre farm with the help of his sons. He was the patriarch of our tribe. He controlled his children, or tried to, all his life and even after he died, or so it seemed. He had five sons; one daughter died in the great flu pandemic of 1918. Named Enoch Benjamin Hoover, my grandfather was known as E.B. to everyone but my grandmother, who called him Bennie. No one ever called him Enoch except the minister who eulogized him at his funeral but who had never known him. Yet, in a peculiar sense, the name Enoch described him best. Enoch, says the religious scholar Elaine Pagels, "far antedates Abraham and Israel's election and, according to Genesis, belongs not to Israel but to the primordial history of the human race." My grandfather was a primordial figure, seemingly fearless, stubborn, opinionated, and patriarchical. Three of his five sons owned farms juxtaposed to his; my father and older uncle lived a few miles away. All were under his sway. My father submitted all his decisions to him for approval, and even we grandchildren were impressed by his great strength, though often awed by his audacity. I recall vividly an argument he had with another horse trader when I was twelve years old, which ended when he told his antagonist that not only could *he* whip him, but if *I* could not do so he would disown me. He carried the day, fortunately for me. That confident strength was immensely assuring. I always felt protected in his presence that seemed rocklike. He was unchanging and as permanent as the land itself.

Born in 1865, grandfather was, at the turn of the century, quite prosperous and soon to become more so. He had a farm and five sons to work his land and additional land to rent if he wished. Moreover the country as well as farmers were prosperous; the period from 1900 to 1914 was a golden age for farmers, so good that their economic position in that era became the standard for "parity," the economic goal of agricultural programs promoted by the federal government beginning with the New Deal.

This agricultural prosperity was a product of several circumstances, most notably the advent of new machinery in the later nineteenth century. While most of the new machines were horse-drawn, they expanded the productivity of those who tilled the soil. The McCormick reaper, for example, enabled farmers to cut oats or wheat much faster than several men could by swinging scythes. Later improvements led to the tying of the cut stems into sheaves. Putting those sheaves into shocks of grain still required much hard hand labor, but the binder, which tied the grain into bundles, reduced the steps necessary to harvest the cereal grains.

The introduction of new machinery did not end the need for extra hands on the farm. Here my grandfather was lucky because of timing. His sons, except for my oldest uncle, B. Frank, were still living at home and by the beginning of World War I were old enough to contribute a full day's work.

During this time my grandfather had enough workers so that he actually filled the role of farm manager while buying and selling horses. My father served as a kind of overseer of his younger brothers—Freeman, Carl, and Dick—who provided the necessary physical labor as they grew older. Working on my grandfather's farm led to a cooperative ethos among the four brothers that continued, to a greater or lesser degree, for most of their adult farming lives.

One of today's common misconceptions is that the family farm, at least as it existed in the early years of the twentieth century, was worked by a farmer with the aid of his wife and perhaps his small children. That farm work required the efforts of several *adults* does not seem to be widely recognized. Some accounts do suggest that farmers, in a spirit of neighborliness, shared efforts; they do not make clear that necessity was the engine for that cooperation.

On the Midwestern farm such as my grandfather's, certain essential work required more than one set of hands. The sheep he raised usually required little care except during lambing time in the spring and the shearing time that followed. The lambs themselves demanded attention at the start—cutting off tails, emasculating males not to be kept for breeding purposes, worming, and so forth. Similar chores were necessary for the farrowed pigs, the calves, and colts. These tasks were onetime affairs that could, and were, done in a relatively short time. But they required at least two sets of hands, one to hold the animal and the other to perform the operation. And not all tasks involved such limited time. The crops raised on a general-purpose farm at the time required more hands as well.

In his most prosperous years my grandfather was extremely fortunate to have the labor of five sons. He also had a farm that was free of mortgages; the times had become prosperous because of America's growth and markets created for American goods by the European war. His business as a horse trader improved immensely at the same time as demand for food and wool also increased. In addition to these efforts, he and his sons raised and sold purebred horses, sheep, and hogs. In the post–World War I year of 1919, the family business grossed $100,000.

But what my grandfather did not know, or few others even suspected, was that times were changing. What seemed to be a permanent path to greater and greater prosperity was merely movement to the crest of a hill. The slide down the other side was steep indeed.

The farm depression began in the 1920s, just as my grandfather's sons had become independent landowners farming their own mortgaged acres. They continued to work his land, but their major concentration had to be on their own farms, three of which adjoined his and had been owned or farmed by relatives. My father's farm was some two miles distant, and my oldest uncle's was an additional three.

All had visions of replicating their father's success, but none was the trader he was. All retained family habits, raising sheep and working together at some tasks. But other practices had either vanished or weakened because of a changing agriculture.

By 1925 all my grandfather's children had married and begun to raise children. Because my father had married late (at thirty-five) in 1924 after living alone for four years, I had cousins who were almost as old as I was. Thus I always felt part of a larger extended family consisting of uncles, aunts, and cousins in addition to my parents and sisters.

My grandfather helped foster that attitude with his paternalism and his nineteenth-century sense of family control. He visited his five sons' farms frequently without warning and offered advice without being asked. He encouraged his sons to farm, often against their talents and inclination, and passed judgment upon their activities.

Not only did I grow up on what was essentially a nineteenth-century farm, I did so with that century's attitudes.

SPRING

*Planting corn: the farmer sets the stake to anchor the check-wire
that trips the planter and allows corn kernels to drop. The disk
attached to the planter arm marks the location of the next row.*

⚜ AS THE FROST left the ground, spring was the mud season. This did not happen all at once; the ground alternately froze and thawed as the weather cooled or heated up. The depth of the mud depended on the depth of the frost or, later in April, on the amount of the spring rain. It also depended upon how much dirt the animals had stirred up in the holding pens next to the outbuildings. That in turn depended upon how long the animals had been confined in those lots during the winter and early spring. As a result, the mud could be ankle high or almost knee high, and it consisted not only of dirt but also of manure, urine, and other nasty ingredients. Overshoes often proved inadequate to the task of navigating through the mud; it was time for rubber boots.

The mud added to the chores, particularly milking the cows. Their tails often dragged in the mud, and in cold spells the bushes at the end of the tails froze into hard clumps that stung when they hit you across the face or in the eyes—which they rarely failed to do. Their udders were a muddy mess that had to be cleaned before milking, a difficult task without running water. Their teats remained as likely to be chapped as they were in mid-winter and required the continued use of Bag Balm. The regime became so distasteful to me that I lost my appetite for milk, particularly warm milk, and have never found it again.

The other animals were less caked with mud and not as much of a problem. As the weather warmed, the horses began shedding, and the mud balls they accumulated came off as we currycombed the loose hair. The pigs, of course, grew very dirty in the spring mud, but that seemed a normal condition for them. The sheep's legs were muddy, but, again, unless the mud hindered their walking, nothing needed to be done about them. The chickens remained inside, out of the mud, though they were not clean.

Spring brought warmer weather and longer days. That meant fewer clothes worn in fewer layers. It did not mean that long winter underwear went into drawers to be taken out the following winter, but it might mean that only one coat sufficed for the walk to school. By the time summer arrived, the longer days with more light allowed us to do the chores without artificial light. The animals required less care and oversight too, except when they were bearing their young.

The date usually used for the end of the threat of a killing frost in our region was May 1. That was the target date for planting corn, which required warm soil to thrive and was quite susceptible to cold weather. Since it was our major crop, our soil preparations looked ahead to that date.

Not that we lacked things to do; that was never a problem on our farm. One crop could be planted in March since its seeds did not freeze. It could lie on the cold ground and even be covered with snow and still germinate. That crop was oats, which served both as a feed for our horses—as well as for cows, sheep, and pigs in limited quantities—and as a cover crop (one that grows rapidly and allows a second crop to flourish underneath) for the next year's hay crop, either alfalfa or, more likely, clover with timothy.

Seedbed preparation and the sowing of the seeds for oats involved several steps. Since the field had usually been used for corn, the residue of cornstalks had to be disposed of in some way. Plowing was not customary as in the preparation of the land for corn or soybeans. The method used instead was disking the land to cut up the stalks into small pieces that would compost easier and not impede the harvesting of the oats or the cutting of the hay in following years. In earlier years when cornstalks were simply burned, preparation was easier. In later years when hybrid corn became standard, seedbed preparation became easier as breeders bred for shorter but nonetheless stronger stalks.

Disking also helped level the field. Cultivation of corn in the preceding crop year had ridged up the land. Disking returned the field to a more nearly smooth surface. If disking was not done, harvesting the oats and hay was much more difficult. Cutting oats on uneven ground might clog the cutter bar with dirt while haying on the same surface could give those on the hayrack a wild ride.

In order to eliminate the ridges, the disking operation could not parallel the corn rows since this direction would leave much of the dirt still mounded. So we disked at a forty-five-degree angle, or diagonally, to break down the ridges. We used a double disk with four sections, two each in front and back.

Then the oats went into the disked soil through an end gate seeder that broadcast the seed by means of a four-bladed fan that spun when turned by a chain belt fixed to the rear axle. The seed mixture in the hopper fed down by gravity and spread for a distance of twelve to sixteen thirty-eight-inch rows on either side. The entire procedure took at least two persons to do the job, one to drive the team and the other to keep the seed hopper full. Usually I tended the hopper.

No further cultivation of the oat crop was required. It was cut and threshed in the summer, the oats were put in storage for winter feed, and the straw was removed from the field to be used as bedding. Alfalfa or clover would grow unimpeded that year, and the next spring it would be cut for hay.

This crop-rotation technique was a variant of an older system dating back to the Middle Ages, except that it raised a crop in a field that in earlier times would have lain fallow. The rotation my father used was based on a five-year cycle. The first year the crop was oats, the next two it was clover hay, and the next two years corn, the real cash crop. Sometimes he extended the cycle to six or seven years with more crops of corn or one of soybeans, depending upon the season and the need for a cash crop. The advantage of the system lay in its variety of crops. A monocultural system with the same crop year after year, as is now common because of economic pressures and artificial fertilizer, risks depleting the soil and exposing the crops to diseases and persistent parasites. This happens despite the repeated applications of fertilizers and pesticides. The older system relied upon crop change and green manure (the plowed-up hay field) together with animal manure to help combat parasites and retain fertility.

In addition to planting oats, another task that needed to be accomplished in the cooler weather of early spring was the pruning of fruit trees. Father had two small but separate plots for trees, one for apples and pears and the other for peaches and cherries. These had to be pruned and shaped while still dormant. This could have been done in the fall, but other, more pressing work then frequently crowded out these tasks.

As with every farm family, and most small-town ones, we had a substantial garden, one devoted primarily to vegetables. Each spring Father plowed a plot in front of our house, one that had been fertilized by animal manure over the winter, with our team of horses and a single walking plow. The garden's fence made the use of our tractor, even after we had one, impractical because of limited turning space, so the working of the soil was done either by horses or by spade and rake. The garden consisted of two perennial beds, strawberries and asparagus, and annual plantings of peas, beans, tomatoes, radishes, onions, cabbage, lettuce, potatoes, watermelon, and squash. This always produced too many fresh vegetables for us to eat, so one of my mother's tasks was to can the surplus for winter. In particular she canned tomatoes by the bushel as well as sweet corn that, unlike the tomatoes, grew alongside regular field corn. These two preserved vegetables were the staples of our winter diet. She also put up many Mason jars of meats, usually beef but sometimes sausage or pork, which filled the half-cellar under the main part of our house along with the home-cured hams and bacons hanging from the rafters.

I disliked the cellar with its dirt floor and musty smell. One of my tasks as a child was to go to the cellar to fetch a jar or other portion of food. The cellar was always damp, and it was always dark even after the house was wired for electricity. Despite my mother's skill at canning, some jars never sealed properly and, as a consequence, spoilage was ever present. But unlike my grandmother, who was less concerned about possible poisoning from somewhat questionable food, my mother would throw out suspect food in the spring, a chore that often fell on me. I would take the jars with bulging lids or an apparent mold on the top of exposed vegetables to our small woods and empty them there to decay, away from our domestic animals. Most of the problems were with canned corn; the tomatoes had enough acid to remain unspoiled.

Chickens provided the meat for our table in late spring and summer. They were fryers—we rarely ate older chickens—that also provided the main meat for company and threshing crews. The males (father or me) caught the chicken by using a metal rod with a hooked end that fit over its leg. Then we killed the chicken by wringing its neck or chopping off its head. It was at this point that Mother took over—unless there were several chickens involved—to scald, pluck, and dismember the bird.

This became the remembered routine, though it was not common among members of our extended family. Grandfather killed his chickens by shooting them, his Indian game chickens so nearly wild that they were virtually impossible to catch. Aunt Fern caught and killed chickens herself; she wrung their necks with an almost professional alacrity. She had no children and crossed the line between masculine and feminine into male territory more than anyone I knew. She went fishing with worms in her apron pocket and put her catch of small fish in the other.

Spring increased the amount of night work on the farm because it was the season for birth. Most domestic animals delivered their young in the spring, for reasons both natural and planned. With wild animals, cool weather brings hormonal change leading to increased sexual drive that results in spring calving or lambing. Births in the spring mean the young are more likely to survive as they can gain enough strength in the summer to live through the upcoming cold winter. But because farmers could control animal breeding, they had a better idea of exactly when births would occur. They could prepare for these events and space them between other periods of intensive labor.

The shorter gestation period of pigs and sheep seemed naturally to call for breeding in the fall and birthing in the spring. With pigs, their faster growth allowed for two litters each year. This was uncommon among sheep, though the reason why is still unclear to me. I always assumed that one factor, at least in our area, was the lack of taste for lamb. Our market for lamb centered on Eastern markets in November and December while pork, bacon, and ham sold well the year round.

We knew when our ewes would lamb, at least within a few days, not just by their distended flanks but also because of the breeding record. The ram wore a canvas harness on his chest that contained a colored powder or had a colored chalk rubbed onto it. In either case the bred ewe had been marked and her due date recorded.

There was no similar system for pigs. As a consequence the pregnant sows and ewes both had to be watched carefully as they neared delivery. Much could go wrong—problems with the birth process or with the first few hours of life.

With animals the normal delivery is head first, just as in humans, but sometimes the fetus is turned so that the breech is first, making for a difficult, if not impossible, delivery. The best remedy is to turn the fetus into the proper position by inserting a hand up the birth canal into the womb and manipulating the fetus to a head-first position.

Breech delivery could occur in any animal from sheep to horses. In larger animals the veterinarian or a knowledgeable adult performed the operation. In smaller animals, adult hands proved too large for the procedure. My father, in particular, had huge hands that were obviously unsuitable to the task. This meant that I had to do it.

While awkward deliveries such as these were thankfully rare, we owned one ewe that had habitual problems because she had once suffered an accident while heavily pregnant. We had found her struggling on her back, unable to turn over and regain her feet. She survived but with permanently damaged muscles that caused her difficulty in pushing her lambs (she usually had twins) over her pelvis. I had to help in most of her deliveries, but we kept her because of her twin births.

More routine work involved ensuring that the mother bonded with the young. In general, animals identify their offspring by smell. The mother sniffs the newly born baby, and the odor remains with her during the time she nurses her young.

Sometimes this bonding does not occur; more often the problem is how to ensure the survival of an orphan or, in the case of pigs, a smaller member of a litter who has been crowded out from an available teat at feeding time. One way of solving this problem is through artificial feeding, that is, bottle training. Another is adoption by a different mother, which depends upon fooling the foster mother's sense of smell. For example, if the surrogate ewe had had a young lamb that died, the skin of the dead animal could be placed on the orphan. In my experience this camouflage never worked very well and certainly was not possible with baby pigs—it was too difficult to skin them. Trying to rub some of the mother's smell onto the baby also failed much of the time. Most orphans, as a consequence, became bottle babies.

With our cows and horses, practices differed. In the first place, we had fewer of each: five to six cows and two mares. This allowed for breeding and time of birth to be closely controlled. With longer gestation periods than sheep or pigs, only one birth per year was likely, and we adjusted the times of birth accordingly.

Calves and colts born in the spring had the advantage of warmer weather and better grass. But they could survive in colder weather if given shelter, and their birth at another time might prove more advantageous to the farmer. For example, in raising calves to sell as feeder stock, those born in the winter would be larger and better able to benefit from the summer's grass than those born later in the spring.

In our case, with a small operation and with our selling mostly sour cream, the calves were of lesser concern. Our main consideration was the price of milk and cream. In the summer, milk production always rose with the grass diet, so there was more for the calves to drink but less cream for us to sell. The creamery, however, lowered the price because the supply had increased. In the winter the supply shrank, but the price rose. In short, the trade-off seemed about even, and our cows calved in the spring.

Our mares too foaled in the spring; once again, the calculations came out about even. Spring foaling involved the dual function of the mares as mothers and as workers. The colts wanted to nurse frequently and became angry if separated too long from their mothers. In turn, the mothers became agitated if they did not have their udders emptied when they began to hurt and if they did not see their colts. Hence nursing mares proved to be more difficult to manage and less available for work. In the winter, with less work to do, the nursing mothers would be better workers and their colts easier to manage, but the colts would require more care.

The result of this juggling act was that we had a variety of young animals born in the spring, animals that required extra care at a time when we also had to prepare for crop planting.

Lambs, pigs, calves, and colts were not the only new animal crop. Early spring saw the arrival of baby chicks in a cardboard carton in the mail. We hatched none of our own chickens; it was cheaper and more convenient to buy them. Besides, all our full-grown roosters had either been eaten or sold in autumn; now only hens occupied our chicken house. The chicks arrived with a few dead and some weak individuals included; but even with the wastage, Father concluded they were a bargain.

The inside of the brooder house contained a kerosene heater under which the small chicks huddled together, but they thrived under it. They drank water from inverted fruit jars with small troughs incorporated into screw-top lids, and ate from a feeder that contained mash purchased from a local feed store. They grew until they were large enough to go outside to scratch for seeds and small insects and eat cracked or whole grain.

When large enough they would replace the older hens, which we would then take to market. The young roosters in the group made up our main meat supply during the summer. Beef and pork canned by my mother, and bacon and ham cured by my father, added to the menu. Our diet changed when electricity came into the house and brought a refrigerator and later a freezer that held steaks, hamburger, and pork chops.

Besides their meat, the chickens laid the eggs that produced part of Mother's household money. The best chickens, or so we thought, were a multi-purpose breed, White Rocks. The best laying hens were the Leghorns that most neighbors raised. They did indeed lay more eggs, but they were smaller birds and less suitable for eating. In that era, most tables featured larger chickens for frying and roasting. Four pounds was an ideal weight for a fryer; the two-and-a-half pounders now common in the marketplace would have been an object of derision when I was young. The larger birds had a more robust, meaty taste that we preferred.

One of the consequences of running a general-purpose farm with a wide array of animals was the presence of, and danger involved in, the male animals that were used to breed the females. These males were aggressive, prone to protecting their females, and likely to attack with or without provocation. But the farmer needed males since there was as yet no artificial-insemination service available in our area.

When I grew up our farm had one ram, one boar, and one bull to service twenty ewes, five to six sows, and about the same number of cows. We favored Shropshire rams, Poland China boars, and Jersey bulls. All were dangerous and had to be carefully watched. The Shropshire ram weighed more than a hundred pounds and liked to butt you when your back was turned. Once, when he was irritated by the loading of lambs into our farm trailer, he ran at me and hit me at the knees, knocking me to the ground. Irate, I swung the tailgate at him with considerable force and hit him squarely on the head. I feared I had killed him, a grand champion ram at the Iowa State Fair, but he seemed not to have been affected.

The Jersey bull we owned had no horns but was a compact bundle of muscle. He too enraged me more than once and provoked me into foolhardiness. After being chased by him into a barn when I was only six, I picked up a pitchfork determined to chase and discipline him. I failed; he chased me back. I think I could have killed him if I had had the strength—or he might have killed me.

Our Poland China boar frightened me more than any other animal. Boars can easily weigh five hundred pounds, and have a formidable set of tusks—quite sharp, wicked-looking, and capable of slashing opponents severely. In our neighborhood, one boar killed a horse by running under him and opening up his abdomen to spill out his intestines. I never felt tempted to challenge the boar's domain and kept well away from it.

The male animals were necessary but posed a danger to the household and were hardly worth the trouble and expense of keeping. They required extra security in pens or stalls strong enough to contain them; they offered only a limited time for their usefulness as breeders. Since most farmers raised young females to replace older females, this meant that the old male could breed his own daughter, a genetically undesirable situation. A new male was needed for each generation.

Sometimes ownership of a male could be avoided by using another's sire. That was our case; we had no stallion even though we had two horses. The reason was simple: the horses belonged to Grandfather and were loaned to us for working and raising mules. He had a jack (a male donkey) that he kept at stud; it attracted much business since its off-spring contained a high percentage of sorrel mules that were in great demand. He loaned us two large, sorrel Belgian mares, and when one was in heat, we took her the two miles to Grandfather's farm to be bred.

My grandfather always had a herd of horses in his pasture. From time to time he bred the mares and traded the others. He kept the jack in a stall in his barn, not permitting him to run with the herd; he was used only to breed with the mares. (My Uncle Frank had a Percheron stallion that weighed nearly a ton and was scary. My cousin Herbert, showing off one day, mounted the horse in the barn and frightened us all.) I believe most stallions were confined like this.

The practice had an amusing consequence. Concerned that he might fail to note when a mare was in heat and al-ways attracted by a bargain, my grandfather bought a crip-pled horse at an auction. The horse was a handsome Spotted Moroccan that had been hit by a railway car but had sur-vived with a damaged hip. So crippled that he could not get up from the ground without someone holding his tail, the horse, or so my grandfather believed, was incapable of im-pregnating his mares. As a result, the horse ran with his mares. Grandfather thought the horse could detect the mares that were in heat but could not service them. He was wrong, as the spotted colts proved.

My mother often described me to her friends as "innocent." I may have looked innocent; old photographs show a
very blond boy with dreamy eyes (I think I was sleepy). But
how could I have been? I helped Grandfather when I took
the mares to his place to be bred, and I could see the animals
breeding all around. Sex was omnipresent, yet rural people
often acted as if it were not. My grandmother, for example,
struck me as Victorian, hesitating even to say "legs" (she said
"limbs" instead) and was shocked by any hint of sexuality.
She seemed far removed from the activity going on by the
side of the barn less than a hundred feet away, even though
she had six children.

The farm animals taught me about more than just sex.
They taught me about dominance and submission, about social hierarchy. Our cows always walked into the barn in the
same order, with the same cow in the lead. One of our two
Belgian mares was clumsy and careless; she lived in fear of
her teammate who continually chased her or made her move
from a spot the dominant mare wanted. One day the fearful
one blundered into a tree trying to escape the bully and dis-
located her shoulder.

One theory holds that domestication occurs only in those
animals that practice dominance and submission instinc-
tively. The alpha animal signals its dominance by baring
teeth and laying its ears against its head (in the case of cows
and horses). This behavior has entered the language: someone who submits to another is "cowed."

The new generation of animals required special care to
make them more self-sufficient before corn-planting time.
They needed to learn to eat grain and grass, and they needed
to be inoculated against disease. The pigs needed to lose
their needle teeth; the lambs needed their tails docked. All

the male animals except those kept for breeding purposes needed to be castrated.

Some observers believe that these latter operations involve needless cruelty. In fact this is not the case with these painful but necessary procedures. Take for example, the cutting of lambs' tails. In some regions of the world, lambs become sheep with tails intact. They live, however, in a different climate under different conditions than exist in the Midwest.

Sheep farmers were chiefly concerned with insect infestations in the stained wool of a sheep's rear end. Under even normal circumstances, feces and urine stained the hindquarters when an animal relieved itself because it could raise its tail only so high. The waste-soaked area then became the target of flies that laid eggs. The resulting maggots caused much irritation and discomfort to the animals, causing weight loss and poorer health. The farmer had to shear off the wool in the infested area, brush away the maggots, and apply ointment to repel flies. But it was far better to prevent the trauma by eliminating the tail.

An even worse plague was the screwworm that came north from Texas. Spread by another variety of fly, the screwworm differed from the maggot in that it devoured healthy as well as unhealthy flesh. It earned its name from seeming to screw itself into the flesh, from which it was difficult to extract. Sheep also suffered much more pain from the screwworm attack than from ordinary maggots. The most effective remedy required shearing off the wool in the affected region, removing the worms with pliers or tweezers, applying an ether compound to kill those worms that remained, and then coating the area with a black coal-tar compound to aid healing and prevent future infestations.

Docking lambs' tails did not completely prevent maggot or screwworm infestation, but it helped. Castration, on the other hand, promised no special relief for the individual animal; it was entirely for the owner's advantage. He received two benefits from the procedure: the animals became more docile, and they brought a higher price when sold for meat.

Meat from male animals had a stronger flavor than did that from neutered ones, and it was discounted if the animal had not been castrated or if the procedure had been done after the animal had matured. Market reports included prices for the latter under the label of "stag."

Since our lambs and pigs were most likely to wind up in the slaughterhouse, we castrated them when they were a few weeks old because they could more easily be controlled and the shock to the animal was not as great.

The anguished cries of the animals as my father first cut off the end of the scrotum and then stripped the outer tissue from the testicles before pulling them out stay with me to this day. Could I ever bring myself to do that? Yet I knew that my father tried to be as gentle as possible; others reportedly bit off the testes with their teeth (the testicles were slick and difficult to hold).

A neighbor's example prompted the notable exception to our castrating pigs when young. He had bought some young boars that probably weighed 150 pounds each. He then castrated them in the belief that after they recovered and gained enough weight, he could sell them at the highest price to an unsuspecting packer for nonstag prices. He resorted to an old remedy, kerosene, dating back to the nineteenth century, to be used to treat the castrated hog. As a result, I found myself observing the spectacle of a middle-aged man chasing hogs around his feed lot squirting kerosene from an oil can on his squealing victims. Little did I know that such a person soon would be me.

My father decided to try this kind of husbandry and bought some half-grown boars. He instructed me to hold each animal as he operated, an assignment even tougher than it sounds. To hold immobile a pig that weighed as much as I did while he struggled desperately to free himself proved almost impossible. So too did trying to spray kerosene on the swollen rear end of the animals as they ran to avoid the stinging liquid. The project proved profitable but was never repeated, to my great relief.

I had always wondered where the stronger-flavored meat of such animals appeared after it was processed. I never saw it advertised as such in any store, but I finally found the answer years later when touring New Zealand and spending the night in a bed-and-breakfast on a farm. The woman who operated it had a herd of yearling bulls in one pasture, and I asked her about their intended use, thinking there must have been quite a demand for breeding stock for her to keep so many males. She told me that she contracted to sell them to a fast-food chain to use in its hamburgers. The chain had determined that a certain percentage of the stronger-flavored meat made its burgers taste better. So there it was: our stags had probably ended up in sausage.

By April when the weather had warmed, it was sheepshearing time for our small flock. We had manual sheep shears that were used to trim around the eyes and rear ends, but using these handheld shears to cut off an entire fleece would have taken a long time and produced indifferent results. Instead we hired a team of professional shearers.

Since the flock was small, these shearers fit our job in between larger ones, making us dependent upon their schedule. I looked forward to the work as a break in the everyday routine and a chance to meet different people. The two men arrived with their equipment: a small gasoline engine that drove a series of arms ending in a pair of shears with a sliding cutter blade, and a grindstone. The grindstone served to sharpen the blades that became dull rather quickly as they peeled off the wool. Except for the engine, the basic equipment was vintage nineteenth century; my grandfather's shed contained rusty clippers that differed mainly from the newer equipment by being hand-cranked. Had I lived in his day, I probably would have had to furnish the power. But my task at the time was different: I got to stand in the wool sack to pack down the fleece with my feet.

The routine was as follows. A shearer would grab a sheep and set it upright between his knees. Beginning by shearing the belly, he would cut the wool off the legs next and finish off with the sides and back. He would then roll up the fleece and tie it securely while my father treated any cuts on the sheep with antiseptic before releasing the animal. Someone would hand the fleece to me as I stood in the wool sack, a large burlap bag held in place by a wooden frame.

Our flock consisted of Shropshire sheep, a multi-purpose breed that were used mostly as a meat animal. They produced a smaller amount of wool than those animals bred for wool—seven or eight pounds as compared with ten to twelve harvested from breeds such as Columbias and Merinos. Shropshire wool was graded as coarse while that of heavier wooled breeds was classified as fine, having more fibers and being better suited for making cloth.

We raised sheep primarily for their meat as Australian competitors proved too strong to allow wool growing to be profitable as an important source of income. American wool had been competitive in the nineteenth century, but that was before synthetic fibers and when most American mills relied upon domestic sources for their raw materials. We still sheared the sheep for a little extra income and to add to the animals' comfort in a hot Midwestern summer, but the amount of money the wool brought was insignificant.

I took the fleeces handed to me and tramped them down into the bag until it was solidly full. It then resembled a six-to eight-foot sausage in a burlap bag and might weigh several hundred pounds. The wool sack had changed little over the centuries from its origins in England and its prominent place as a seat cushion for members of Parliament. We hauled the sacks to town to be sold to a dealer in hides, wool, and scrap metals. The firm, Bernstein and Son, had been in Oskaloosa for years, and provided a living for one of the few Jewish families there.

My entire skin, the exposed parts anyway, benefited from this work as the lanolin from the fleece softened and smoothed it. A less desirable consequence appeared at night when I undressed to take a bath or go to bed. What I believed were ticks would congregate on my belt or sock line. I greatly dreaded removing them, fearing Rocky Mountain Spotted Fever, but they never seemed embedded and came off easily. Only years later did I learn from a tick expert that they were not ticks at all but a variety of fly. The insects dotted the skins of the sheared sheep.

The animals happily ran and jumped after being freed of their wool. They milled around, particularly ewes and their lambs, trying to reestablish the old familiar bond of smell. The wool had never been washed and contained all the odors accumulated since the time of the lamb's birth. Shearing altered the smell of the animals somewhat, causing confusion in the one sense that provided identity.

I never sheared a sheep at home; my job kept me in the wool sack. I did, however, actually clip one at the Iowa State Fair when I was showing sheep there. As I sat on our trunk containing tools and supplies, the kind that every exhibitor had, watching the crowds move up and down the aisles, an official in the sheep barn whom I knew asked me to be a contestant in a sheep-shearing contest. I protested that I had never actually shorn a sheep, but he persisted, saying he had failed to recruit many contestants and that the contest was important in helping advertise the sheep business to fairgoers. I reluctantly agreed.

My experience as an observer failed to serve me well in this contest that fortunately attracted few spectators. Imbued with a goal to get the fleece off in one piece and not to cut or otherwise injure the poor sheep, I took what seemed to me to be an inordinate amount of time to shear the animal. But I succeeded and even placed third in the contest—out of three contestants.

No good deed goes unpunished is the old maxim that applied in this case. Although I received no tangible reward for my performance—no ribbon, no certificate of achievement, and certainly no money—another exhibitor approached me the next day with a request: Would I shear some of his sheep? Impressed with my care, or so he said, he wondered if I were in the business. I informed him that I had retired.

Sheepshearing occupied but a small place in the major work of the spring. That work involved preparation and planting of the major crop, corn and/or soybeans. In most seasons we did not plant soybeans. Our income came from animal sales; the animals ate the crops we raised. We did not sell the corn we raised but quite often bought corn to supplement it. Father's theory was that feeding the crops to animals meant the return of fertility to the soil through their manure as well as being labor saving.

The main crop was corn because this grain has a high carbohydrate or energy content and animals liked it. But some characteristics of corn had to be taken into account. For one,

it had a longer growing season than the fallback crop, soybeans. Farmers planted their corn after May 1 when the danger of frost no longer threatened the tender crop. But if it
was still cold or if it had been rainy and the soil could not be
tilled soon enough, planting might be delayed until June.
Such late planting ran the risk of the corn failing to mature
by the first frosts of autumn. In that circumstance the corn,
still full of moisture, often rotted or otherwise spoiled.

In the case of a delayed planting season, soybeans became the substitute crop. Planted in June, they ripened by
October, in plenty of time to be harvested. And they brought
a good price when sold. But farmers did not feed soybeans to
their livestock in the belief that such feed produced inferior
meat. Besides, the dried bean was difficult to digest. Instead
soybeans became part of the animals' diet in the form of soy-
bean oil meal, a protein supplement. This addition came
from commercial sources as we lacked the equipment to extract the oil.

Corn could also be difficult to digest for livestock, particularly cattle and sheep with four stomachs suited to high
fiber and coarse diets. One way to help them digest the kernels was to crack them into small pieces in a hammer mill.
To make the most of the corn, farmers ran pigs in with the
livestock to eat the partially digested kernels that the animals secreted. Now organic farmers have rediscovered this
method as they allow hogs to mingle with cows to root in the
latter's feces.

No other crops competed with corn or soybeans as cash
crops, but sometimes we did grow alternatives. I remember
growing wheat one year and barley still another. Both were
excellent crops but not suited to our situation. Farmers who
raised horses liked barley and thought it superior to corn,
but the yield of grain per acre was less, and barley's beards

made it difficult and unpleasant to harvest. Its straw was not suitable for bedding.

Both humans and animals liked wheat, and it grew well in the Midwest. Why not raise it? There were several reasons. It lacked a regional market and local grain elevators specialized in corn. Midwestern wheat farmers could not compete with those on the Great Plains who benefited from economies of scale. And wheat often had to be cracked first in order to be used for feed and lacked the caloric content of corn.

Both wheat and barley had been more popular in earlier eras when people made their own bread or brewed their own beer. Now they were novelty crops for us, crowded out by corn and soybeans.

I have a few memories about these particular grains. One winter we ate some of the wheat we had raised as breakfast cereal. It tasted good on cold mornings, but the kernels required long soaking, at least overnight, to become palatable. I do not remember ever eating barley, but I do remember the terrible itching and scratching that barley beards induced whenever I went into the field or when we threshed the crop. It seemed as if the beards lodged everywhere—in socks, overalls, and even underwear.

The main task in getting ready for corn planting was to prepare the soil. This was a three-step process. Plowing was first and could be done either in the fall after the corn harvest or in the spring. Opinions divided as to which was the superior practice. Fall plowing had several advantages: the work could be done when there was more time available than in the busier spring, and the winter freezing and thawing broke up the clods and allowed the soil to collect more moisture. The major disadvantage was soil erosion, caused by wind and water, that came with the loss of any ground cover.

After plowing, usually in the spring for us, disking broke up the soil and leveled it out. The round metal disks had sharp edges that rolled over the ground, cutting up leftover clods or clumps of grass or pieces of cornstalks left on the surface. Disking required less power than plowing and could be done much more quickly. Plowing with horses or with the early row-crop tractors allowed the use of no more than two fourteen-inch bottoms (plowshares that cut the soil), which meant that each trip down the field covered a width of no more than twenty-eight inches. Even two horses could pull an eight-foot disk with ease, and a small-size tractor could manage one that was twelve feet.

The final step in preparing the seed bed involved harrowing. This reduced the soil lumps even more than the disking and left the ground as smooth as possible. The tool here consisted of several square sections of teethed frames attached to long pieces of wood (usually a two-by-six of varying lengths) by a hook-and-loop arrangement that provided flexibility in the size of the implement. We usually put three four-foot sections in one harrow to cover about twelve feet on each pass.

Harrowing required the least power and was the easiest of the three tasks. Unlike the earlier procedures that penetrated into the soil, harrowing only scratched the surface. While most plows and disks had seats for the driver (an exception was the horse-drawn plow, of which there were both walking and riding versions), the structure of harrows made riding unlikely when working with horses. The driver usually walked; and without the weight of a driver, horses had an easy time.

Plowing required considerable skill, as plowing contests at the time demonstrated. As a consequence, a boy learned that step in the process last. Disking demanded less skill; harrowing asked for the least.

I began at the bottom, walking behind a three-section harrow when I was still quite young. I soon learned, however, that I needed more than a little skill to negotiate turns at the fenced ends of the field. Turning to reverse directions could be, and was, my problem. Too abrupt a turn would flip one section of the harrow upside down, twisting the entire imple-ment over on itself.

One day when I overturned the harrow, the half-broken team (one not fully trained to work) panicked and bolted, breaking the harness in their escape. (Since it was the de-pression, the harness had not been replaced and was rotted. My father regularly patched the broken reins and other pieces with copper rivets.) The horses did not stop in their flight: they crashed through two solid wooden gates and ran down an adjoining highway. The clapping of their huge hooves on the concrete could be heard for half a mile. This was not my last incident with these horses; the combination of unruly teams and old equipment tripped me on other occasions.

My father never permitted me to carry out the final step and plant the corn; that task required more skill and prac-tice than I had. But his restriction was not unusual. Some middle-aged men were not allowed by their fathers to drive the planter.

Before the advent of herbicides and insecticides, the most pressing problem in corn culture was weed control. This had to be done by intensive cultivation—digging weeds out by their roots. To make this possible, the corn had to be planted in a pattern that best aided cultivation. That pattern was a checkerboard, which allowed a two-row cultivator, drawn either by horses or attached to a small tractor, to go north and south and then east and west.

Planting that pattern, however, demanded precision. Rows must be aligned in each direction. Corn must be planted in hills (all kernels in the same spot), not drilled in a continuous row. Rows must be straight, not contoured. Within these constraints, limited variation could be allowed for the distance between rows, the number of seeds in each hill, and so forth.

How was this to be done? My father used a two-row, horse-drawn planter all his life; he had learned how to use this tool with considerable success. To ensure that each hill of corn had three or four kernels (depending upon such factors as soil quality) he would insert plates with different-size openings in the bottom of the two boxes containing the seed corn. These hoppers rested atop steel runners that ran several inches under the soil. To make sure the rows had the proper alignment, he used a wire guide that ran the length of the field. The wire guide tripped the seed plate at proper intervals across the field while at the same time an arm extended from the right side of the planter to mark the location of the next row. If done properly, the hills of corn lined up both lengthwise and crosswise in the field. All this resulted in a nice grid that viewed from above must have looked like a checkerboard.

As is characteristic of most solutions, this one led to unanticipated problems. The straight rows on Iowa's rolling fields resulted in increased erosion. No contoured fields and few grassy waterways impeded the loss of valuable topsoil.

Work did not end with the planting of corn. We awaited the sprouting of the seeds and the emergence of new plants. Wet areas where plants had drowned needed to be reseeded. This we did by hand. Sometimes a cutworm attack forced us to eliminate whole sections because they lacked the number of plants to ensure a substantial yield. This meant getting out the planter again to reseed.

New plants demanded cultivation, in two rows at a time and in the same direction as the planting. My father did this by a two-row riding cultivator; when I became old enough, I did it with a tractor. In each case the cultivator consisted of several shovels that plowed the ground between two rows. The first cultivation had to be done slowly so as not to cover the small plants or tear up others at the edges of the field. At the same time the tiny weeds that persisted even after plowing, disking, and harrowing needed to be eliminated. The second cultivation went the width of the field while the third went lengthwise a second time.

By the first of June the corn was a few inches high; it would require two more cultivations before it grew too tall for the cultivator.

Spring officially ended on June 20. The days were growing not only longer but also warmer. Much work remained ahead. We hoped the corn would be "knee high by the Fourth of July," the end of cultivation.

Today all this has changed. Contour planting has supplanted checkerboard planting, and herbicides have practically ended cultivation. Corn "drilled" in rows (as opposed to planted) permits more seeds per acre, and the end of cultivation means that the height of the corn is important only for marking its seasonal growth.

My grandparents and their family circa 1908.
My father is in the middle of the back row.

Respite: A Family Farm

❦ IN 1920, at the mature age of thirty, my father left home to move to his mortgaged farm. For four years he lived alone in an old house on the hundred-acre farm, physically removed from his four brothers and his strong, even overpowering, father. He did not, however, break the emotional dependency upon his father. He continued to rely on him for advice in most decisions.

The farm Father bought was one typical of the Midwest in that era. It was an all-purpose farm designed for a variety of crops and animals, divided into a number of small fields separated by woven or barbed-wire fences and containing an unexpectedly large number of outbuildings. Designed to be cultivated by horses and to supply different feed for a variety of animals, the small parcels were ill suited to the mechanization of agriculture in the 1940s and 1950s. They lacked the space for large equipment to be used for the best advantage. And while the land was rich Iowa soil, because it lay between two rivers it was subject to erosion.

Horses provided the major source of power for field work in the spring. The early tractors and (barely) mobile steam

engines were too heavy and clumsy to do much field work—
disking, harrowing, or cultivating. Their weight packed the
soil too hard, and their size made them unsuitable for cultivating row crops. They were primarily useful, at least
on smaller Midwestern farms, for stationary belt work—
providing power for a saw or threshing machine. But the cost
of a steam engine with limited use was prohibitive for the av-
erage small farmer. Such an engine most often belonged to a
ring of farmers who also owned a threshing machine in common and who threshed small grains such as oats, wheat, and
barley for its members. The Hoover brothers belonged to
such a ring. Early gasoline-powered tractors were less expensive and cumbersome, but they were ill fitted to much field
work again because of their size and shape. They could, and
were, used for similar tasks as the steam engines.

All the tasks of disking, harrowing, cultivation, or planting could best be accomplished by the more nimble horses
and horse-drawn equipment. Plowing was another matter. It
required more power to turn the surface soil over as prevailing agricultural theory prescribed, an approach probably derived from earlier days of breaking the prairie sod. It could
be and was done by horses, but in order to complete the task
in less time it required the effort of more than just a two-
animal team. A pair of horses could manage to pull a one-
bottom (one plowshare) plow, but any larger implement
called for an additional two or more work horses. Even
though the additional team delivered twice the productivity,
it still was slower work than that produced by the heavy
tractor. So we used the tractor.

I cannot recall my father ever plowing the fields with
horses as he did our family garden. My memory of the horses
we used and the tools we had is still vivid. We never employed more than a team of two horses, or mules, though we

did raise mules to sell and we did briefly have a Western horse for my sister and I to ride to school. My memory of tools is clear because I played with them while growing up.

As was the case on many other farms, old pieces of equipment lay around in the open subject to sun and rain, some abandoned for newer models and some stored outside because there was no other place to put them. Although the farm had many other buildings, it lacked a machine shed; as a consequence, disks, plows, and cultivators, mostly horse-drawn, lay out in the open, their blades covered with axle grease to prevent rust. There was no multi-bottom plow.

Horses were available in large numbers when my father began farming on his own, and my father could cooperate with my grandfather in training horses while he worked the land. He owned no horses to my knowledge but relied instead on those loaned him by his father.

My grandfather found himself in a very favorable situation at this time. He had always been a horse trader; he liked horses as much as his father liked sheep. He bought and sold horses, making up matched teams for buyers and supplying animals for other purposes. He had built a reputation for his knowledge of horses, and he tried them out for a local auction barn. In this capacity he evaluated soundness, physical health, and potential for work. As a result of his knowledge he received calls from many horse buyers.

The building and surfacing of roads demanded by the rapid increase in automobiles required the work of horses. Much of the road-building equipment was horse-drawn, so contractors needed many draft horses for their work, and that practice continued until World War II. Even after the more frequently traveled roads were paved, secondary roads had to be maintained, and horses still were used to do this. Growing up, I can remember my father satisfying his poll tax by working on the dirt road that passed beside our farm. The time required to work depended upon what equipment my father furnished. If he brought his team and a slip to move dirt, it was one day; if he worked alone, it was twice that. (The slip moved dirt to fill ruts and smooth out the roads' surfaces.)

Although highway construction created a greater demand for horses, far more of a factor in the rising prices for draft animals had been World War I. The war decimated the European horse population. As a result, the Allies turned to the United States for resupply. When the United States entered the war, the U.S. Army also needed many more horses to pull supply wagons, artillery, ambulances, ammunition caissons, and other vehicles.

When my father died I inherited some of Grandfather's correspondence. In one letter a road contractor asked him for horses, specifying the number of teams he wanted, the characteristics of the horses, size, age, and so forth, and the price he was willing to pay.

Even in the year (1926) I was born, the physical shape of the farm was changing. That year the Iowa Highway Commission had won a court battle based on eminent domain to construct a state highway through my father's farm. It was not an easy victory; Iowa law had not permitted the state to use that right to take two kinds of property, graveyards and orchards. When he bought the farm, my father, who liked trees, especially apple and pear trees, had planted an orchard that was in the projected path of the highway, and he had successfully defended against the construction of a highway on those grounds. The Iowa legislature changed the law, however, rendering his defense no longer viable. The highway went through, eliminating the orchard.

The action of the Iowa Highway Commission was not the first to alter the physical division of the farm into oddly shaped fields. That belonged to the Minneapolis to St. Louis (M&St.L) Railroad. But by the time US 63 was built, the railroad ran few trains on this line, and the infrequent interurbans between Oskaloosa and Cedar were just about bankrupt.

The Northwest Ordinance had set the pattern for land development in the Midwest by surveying rectangular plots of land that presupposed farm fields would be laid out with four sides and regular fence lines. This did not necessarily occur. In some places, natural obstacles—rivers or forests, for example, dictated nonrectangular development; or man-made obstacles such as roads and canals prevented square corners. The latter was what happened in our case. The construction of US 63 in the 1920s gave the farm three triangular fields, two on the west side of the highway and one on the east. The one on the east had been rectangular, but the road had cut off one corner. The two remaining cropland fields were triangular in shape, as was our pasture.

Thus only three of our cultivated fields were four-sided, and one of these had a woodlot that occupied a small irregular area at one end, so it was not really rectangular either. As a consequence, farming the fields involved long rows at one end that tapered into short rows at the other. The corners of the acute angles of the triangle were no more than a few feet long. With horses, short rows presented few difficulties. With tractors, there was almost no room to turn around.

The highway further limited the use of the eastern field for anything but field crops. The plot had originally been equipped for animals since it had a well and a pump to water livestock. After the arrival of the highway, two difficulties became apparent in the use of the field for livestock. With the infrequent trains, animals could be driven across the tracks daily without harm; but that could not be done against the heavy automobile traffic. Neither cows nor horses could be pastured there.

Moreover, the family that had previously owned the farm, the Gunsalus, had allowed the fences on two sides of the triangular field to deteriorate. Both were overhung with vines, one with hops to be used for brewing beer and the other with Virginia creeper and poison ivy. Neither was hogtight, nor would they contain sheep unless they were replaced.

The third fence was adequate for livestock, but when the railroad abandoned its right-of-way, new fencing was needed to enclose the additional land and to build a gate to allow entrance from the highway.

Replacing the fences was a challenge. Tearing out the old fencing could have painful consequences—being pricked with thorns or, worse, afflicted with poison ivy. My father, when we were clearing one fence row, cut his leg with his axe as it glanced off a root and got a bad case of poisoning from the ivy's juice. The episode gave him an increased sensitivity to any exposure to the plant.

But his case paled beside that of our next-door neighbor's son. Given the chore of cleaning a fencerow that contained poison ivy, he had developed a resistance to the plant's juice on his hands. Unthinkingly, though, he had paused to urinate and had given himself a case of poison ivy on his penis. Afraid to tell his parents, he dosed it with iodine, a treatment that resulted, in his words, in "feeling and seeing blue blazes."

The division of the farm into smaller plots demanded almost constant maintenance of fencing, either because of fence age or because of animals testing its limits. Our farm had three kinds of fencing, each a product of a different era. The oldest consisted of a row of Osage Orange trees that grew together into a supposedly impenetrable barrier replete with thorny branches. The second had been constructed with woven wire and several strands of barbed wire, both stapled into wooden posts. The third substituted steel posts for wooden ones and used wraparound wires to secure the woven and the barbed wire to the posts.

Animals challenged all the fencing. They seemed always to believe that the clump of grass on the other side was greener. Larger animals leaned on the fence and loosened the post or wires to reach the tasty bit. Or they rubbed against it to relieve itches. Sheep would reach through between the top of the woven wire and the lowest strand of barbed wire for their nibbles. Hogs were the worst; their noses were so tough and their instincts to root so strong that they continually tried to tunnel under the wire. Even rings in their noses often failed to deter them. As a consequence, we designated the fields with the weakest fences off limits for pigs.

All the fences required work. The Osage Orange intruded into cropland and required regular pruning to limit its spread. Earlier farmers had planted these thorny trees so thickly that cattle and horses hesitated to try to breach them. The fences also provided excellent cover for wildlife, quail, pheasants, and other less desirable inhabitants such as groundhogs and foxes. I liked them, as did other boys my age, because of their fruit—hedge balls, a round green ball that resembled a grapefruit in size but not in surface texture. A hedge ball had a rough, bumpy skin that was sometimes spotted with milky juice but was nonetheless convenient for throwing at someone else. It had several features—lack of smell, size, and consistency—that made it superior for this purpose to balls of dried horse manure.

The older fences had to be cleared of the weeds that grew on them, particularly those encumbered with poison ivy or hops. Rotten wooden posts needed to be replaced, and sagging wire, both barbed and woven, had to be tightened or refitted. Sometimes gates were in the wrong places and had to be relocated. Gates wide enough for horses and horse-drawn equipment frequently were too narrow for tractors and their attachments.

Making fence became habitual. At the start, the usual materials were wooden posts, cedar or similar wood, which formed the stable support upon which woven wire and two or three strands of barbed wire were stapled. We dug the postholes by hand at intervals of about a rod, sixteen and a half feet. This was an arduous task as the soil on the farm had a hard clay base that resisted the spade. Once dug, the hole had to be filled, and the dirt that had been removed tamped back in around the hopefully upright posts. We used no cement to anchor them. Then, after carefully bracing the corner post, which also served as a gatepost if there was to be a gate, we stretched the wire, beginning with the woven wire and ending with the barbed wire. This we did with a block and tackle that both of us, Father and I, pulled with great effort to make taut.

The height of the wire fence and the location of the posts varied according to the animals to be confined. The fence needed to be high enough to discourage cows and horses from trying to jump over. It could be lower in the case of sheep, but with sheep the space between the barbed and woven wire had to be narrower so that the animals would not try to squeeze their heads in between. Even with care we did not always succeed in eliminating breaches. Bulls sometimes jumped the fence, and sheep often had to be freed from being caught between strands of wire.

When steel posts replaced wooden ones, the resulting fence was not as sturdy, but the process of building it became easier. The steel posts could be set by driving them in with a sledgehammer or a special post driver, a heavy steel piece, weighted on one end and hollow on the other, that slipped over a post. The post driver was then brought down with considerable force on the post in a kind of pumping motion. Once the posts were set, the process of fencing duplicated that with wooden posts, except that the fasteners were heavy wires bent around the posts rather than staples driven into wood.

The steel posts also lent themselves to another type of fencing—the electric fence. This consisted of a single wire attached by an insulator to the post and hooked up to a battery or other source of power. An interceptor device then cycled the electricity on and off. Designed to give animals a mild shock when touched, the electric fence had several obvious advantages: it was portable, easy to install and move, and cheap. It enabled farmers to use parts of a pasture in rotation by frequently moving the posts to new locations. And it could be turned off after animals learned that touching the wire brought a shock. They would then avoid the fence even though it no longer had a charge.

But electric fences were not suitable for all animals, and as a consequence we used them less than we might otherwise have. Wool, for example, unless it was damp, provided a good nonconductor for sheep, which were thus largely impervious to shock until they touched the fence with their noses or other bare spots. Electric fences stymied pigs even less because of their natural tendency to tunnel underneath. A single electric wire provided less of a challenge to that urge than did the more traditional fence, unless it was low enough to force the pig to encounter it directly in a vulnerable spot. There was simply no all-purpose electric fence that would hold all farm animals.

The buildings on the farm were numerous and suited to a general-purpose operation. They seemed best for a semi-subsistence farm and had obviously been added as new conditions warranted. Among the buildings when my father moved in were two barns. One was designed as an animal shelter and feeding site since it contained only a haymow and a hay manger running along the length of a side with no openings. The other side had two large openings but without doors. The other barn also had a haymow, but in addition it contained four horse and eight cattle stalls, a boxlike enclosure for small grain or ground feed and a small corncrib (both of these designed for holding small quantities to feed the horses and cows), and a holding section behind the cattle stalls with mangers for hay. The latter was to shelter the cows in severe or inclement weather. Doors on either side of the barn allowed for cows and horses, and wooden ramps led up to these doors. On the second level was a door to permit hayforks to enter and a window to allow a pulley to be installed and rope to exit.

Besides the barns there were three small grain-storage facilities, all with wooden floors, one of which was rarely used because it was old and not ratproof. A corncrib and a hog house both faced a feedlot on one side and a corral with a scale and a chute behind. Of two chicken houses, one was a brooder house for newborn chicks, the other a henhouse for older chickens. (The name "chicken coop," which is commonly used today to describe what we called a chicken house, was never used in my youth. A chicken coop was a wooden box with a slatted opening at the top, which farmers used to carry birds to market.) Finally, there were a small tool shed and, of course, a house. There was no garage, though we later built one.

All the outbuildings shared certain common features. All, save the hog house that was constructed of red tiles, were wooden and all had been painted white, a color that had faded to a greater or lesser degree over time. Our house and one barn appeared to have been constructed of weathered wood. None was ever painted when I was growing up: my father lacked the money for it.

None of the buildings save the garage we later built had a fixed foundation. All, including our house but not the brooder house, rested upon limestone rocks placed at regular intervals on the ground. Because of this uneven support, the buildings tended to sag as the soil shifted because of freezing and thawing. In the case of our house, the kitchen pulled away from the rest of the structure, leaving a sizable gap between the two elements. The brooder house was on wooden skids that allowed it to be dragged from place to place. (In an ironic twist, when a small tornado hit the farm, the garage was torn from its foundation and hurled onto the highway while the brooder house was just overturned. The other buildings remained intact.)

None of the buildings was electrified until 1937. Work or play at night was accomplished by the light of kerosene lanterns or white gaslights. No building had water piped in, though four wells gave us an ample supply of water. Hand pumps provided the lifting power for three wells, but a two-stroke gasoline engine served to fill the large stock tank located near the barn, which was the main water source for livestock. An electric motor later replaced the engine, but we continued to pump water by hand for the house and from the other two wells as long as we lived there. When we had feeder

calves or lambs that foraged in areas away from the one powered pump, we had to pump water by hand as well. (I hated
this task, particularly on hot summer days. Five hundred
sheep can drink a lot of water.)

The house was old-fashioned and would not have been
out of place in the nineteenth century. It was a frame structure with a partial basement and second story. It was not in-
sulated, nor did it have storm windows or doors; it did have
screens in the summer. It was drafty and cold in the winter,
and, in the upstairs bedrooms, stifling hot in the summer. On
the first floor of the house were a kitchen, a large pantry, a
dining room, a living room, a kind of spare room for different
purposes, and a bedroom. The upstairs contained two bedrooms, one of which was mine.

The house lacked running water and central heat. We
carried water in a bucket into the kitchen and went to the
outhouse to relieve ourselves.

Two iron stoves heated the house in winter, one in the
dining room and another in the kitchen with a connecting
pantry between. These burned either local coal—of poor
quality, full of sulfur and rocks—that my father often
hauled from a nearby mine in a horse-drawn wagon, or wood
cut from dead trees in our own woodlot. We cut the downed
trees into sections that could be dragged near the house
where a rotary saw, powered by a gasoline engine and later a
tractor, cut them into chunks. The chunks would later be
split into pieces that would fit into the fireboxes of the stove,
a job frequently assigned to me.

The rest of the house was unheated in winter; as a result,
only two rooms—the kitchen and the living room—were really comfortable. But they often smelled of sulfurous coal,
which was used at night because it lasted longer, and the

rooms were usually cold in the morning when my father arose to stoke the fire. The closed parlor was unheated except when we had guests, and then we used a small kerosene heater.

The emphasis on barns on a general-purpose farm and the relatively smaller size of corncribs and small grain buildings reflected the prevailing philosophy of agriculture at the time. The farm had two major goals—to provide a significant portion of food for the family and the resident animals, and to earn enough for the family to survive in a capitalistic society. Feeding the horses and cows was the reason behind the large barns, which had to hold the necessary hay, a bulky crop, while the more concentrated cereals required small facilities. The relative size and importance of the barnyard buildings provide an insight into farming aims and, in turn, held up a mirror to land use.

A considerable part of the arable land on a farm had to be devoted to raising crops to feed the horses that pulled the plow or the cows that gave the milk or the pigs and chickens to be eaten. That meant that the farm always needed a pasture, a hay field, and a field for oats or other small grains as well as for the major cash crop, corn. This in turn required separation of the land into smaller fields that could confine the animals and restrict them from eating the other crops (unless, of course, it was the intention to allow them in, as with feeder lambs in the corn or cows pasturing temporarily in the hay field). I estimate that on our hundred-acre farm no more than sixty-five acres could ever be devoted to corn or soybeans as cash crops.

Thus the second aim of the farm, to earn money, simply could not be achieved in a period of farm depression followed by a general depression. Low prices for corn and soybeans,

the major cash crops, as well as for eggs, cream, and meat, returned little money to meet family demands and necessary
expenses.

My father bought his farm after borrowing the money
from his uncle Morris, whose wife was Grandmother's sister
and who was an itinerant Quaker minister with few resources except for his share of his wife's holdings. His
younger brother Freeman borrowed from Uncle Morris as
well. It took more than twenty years for my father to repay
the loan; at times he despaired of ever doing so and asked for
his debt to be reduced. He was refused because my uncle
Freeman had already pleaded for some debt relief and had
gotten it.

My father often thought of abandoning the farm but felt
an obligation to Uncle Morris's family to continue to provide
them with the income they needed by repaying the loan.
Moreover, banks extended credit very cautiously for buying
new equipment, constructing or rehabilitating buildings, or
even buying more land, all keys to a larger income. The best
my father could do was to hold on to what he had, making do
until times changed.

But he was not alone. All his brothers had probably become farmers at exactly the wrong time. Perhaps the most
fortunate were the younger ones since they entered the
1920s decade at a later date, when land prices had retreated
from their immediate postwar highs. All were to face a
twenty-year span of difficult times until the demands of
World War II once more brought prosperity to American
farmers.

But all were luckier than many other farmers. They survived as farmers until ill health forced them to retire.

SUMMER

Loading a hayrack.

SUMMER MEANT FREEDOM, literally and figuratively. School ended with a picnic where parents and neighbors shared their food with the teacher and students. Most of the families came with fried chicken and some kind of Jell-O, either green, with cabbage in it, or red, with bananas or other fruit. We did not have to entertain the crowd nor were we confined inside the school. Outside the men talked about crop conditions and maybe even had a pickup game of ball while inside the women talked of domestic affairs and cleaned the tables. The event ended early in the afternoon so that the men could go to work; to take a whole day away from the fields was uncommon and regarded as a special luxury.

Even though I enjoyed school, I anticipated three months away from classes with great pleasure. I knew the summer would be filled with work, that it would be hot and uncomfortable most of the time. My upstairs bedroom, freezing in winter, became stifling hot in the midst of Iowa's humid summer nights that were so necessary for a good corn crop. But I could accommodate. I did not have to wear shoes, and my heavy work shoes remained in the house except when I was working in the barn or other areas that presented hazards such as broken glass, nails, or splinters, or places with manure and other filth. I had long before shed my winter underwear and now could even shed my shirt. Since I habitually wore bib overalls, I removed my shirt less often than if I had had jeans to wear and could expose my entire chest to the sun.

Hazards limited the extent of this stripping. Any work involving hay or small grains—oats, wheat, or barley— brought with it scratches and itching. The stubble cut feet and ankles without shoes, and the pollen and dust settled everywhere on bare and clothed bodies alike. Even corn- fields hurt as the leaves, if you brushed against them, cut as badly and hurt as much as paper cuts. Despite minor cuts and scratches, I persisted in going barefoot in the summer until I graduated from high school, but I went bare-chested less frequently.

Two major tasks occupied the month of June, haying and cultivating corn. When the hay crop matured, the crucial time occurred when the uncut hay was still green enough to be palatable to the livestock but not so green that it would rot, mold, or even catch fire when stored in a barn or stacked. Thus the time of the first hay crop depended upon the season, the weather, and the type of hay.

Haying required a minimum of three steps. The first was to mow the hay crop. All mowers, horse-drawn or tractor- pulled, shared the same basic principle. A cutter bar with sharp triangular blades moved in a sliding motion over a sta- tionary bed, cutting the stems of the hay as they were guided onto the cutter bar by teeth extending forward from the bed. The bar could be raised or lowered to accommodate changes in the ground level, or to negotiate turns, or to go through gates and along roads. But as any person mowing highway shoulders or ditches knows, in practice the task is never easy.

In the first place, the ground in the fields was never com- pletely even but was often filled with holes and covered with bumps occurring naturally or thrown up by animals.

Groundhogs were particularly active in this digging. Sometimes rocks or other hard objects found their way into the hay field.

Nor was this the only hazard. Tangled weeds or pieces of cornstalk left over from the preceding year's crop often clogged the cutter bar and brought the mowing to a halt. These impediments required removal from the cutting teeth by hand, which could be tricky with a nervous, half-broken team likely to stampede if bitten by a horsefly. Some of the more rigid clogs might even break a blade, stopping the mowing until a new blade could be found and riveted in.

The next step in the process was the curing of the hay, either lying on the ground or raked up into a windrow. The hay lying flat on the ground drew moisture from the ground as well as being dampened by dew. When somewhat drier, it needed to be raked into rows in order to be picked up more easily as well as to dry further.

We used two kinds of raking machines. The first, a dump rake, had slowly been phased out. As the name suggests, it picked up the hay in its curved tines in a straight line, carried it a few feet, and then dumped it when the operator pulled a lever. The driver's main problem was to create a straight row of hay: he had to be skillful enough to dump at the proper moment. Replacing the dump rake, left to rust in the corner of a lot, was the side-delivery rake. It required less judgment on the part of the operator because no dump was necessary. Instead the diagonal rake continually discharged the hay from its side into a windrow (hence the name "side delivery"). The driver might still have a crooked trail of hay if he were not paying attention to the direction of the team of horses, but the prospect was less likely.

The hay cured in the windrow until it was dry enough for storage. Rain frustrated the process and spoiled the hay's quality. Enough rain would ruin it entirely, and farmers tried hard to make hay while the sun shone.

I remember one occasion at Uncle Carl's farm when we had worked putting up hay all day but stopped when the sun went down so that we could return home to do our evening chores. My aunt advised my uncle that rain had been forecast, and indeed lightning flashed and thunder rumbled in the west. Worried that the hay remaining in the field would be ruined, he asked us to try to finish the work. We went home, did our chores, and returned to continue haying. We finished at two in the morning after eighteen hours of hard physical work broken only by meals and other temporary respites. The rains never came.

If the hay in the windrow was wet, it had to be turned over to speed drying. In any case, when it was sufficiently dry the storing of hay began—the last step. This never commenced before mid-morning, nine-thirty or ten, by which time the dew had evaporated.

We used three methods for storing the hay: loose, baled, and cut. The first two methods had a long history in agricultural practice; the last was a temporary experiment that failed, at least for us.

Farmers had put loose hay into barns and haystacks for years. The changes wrought by technology had not much altered the method. Instead of pitching the hay from rows in the field with pitchforks, a hayloader transferred the hay to the wagon. Instead of pitching the hay in the barn, a system utilizing a track and a series of pulleys carried large bunches into the haymow.

Harvesting loose hay was not a one-man task because of restraints imposed by time, curing weather, and storage arrangements. One man could cut a field of hay and rake it into rows in an efficient and timely way using horse-drawn equipment. But the next steps became more complicated. As noted earlier, the mown crop needed to dry enough so that it did not spoil or heat up enough to ferment and catch fire when put into a stack or a barn, while at the same time it needed to remain palatable—not so dry that animals would refuse to eat it.

One man could not manage to harvest a whole field of hay at once unless it was very small. He could conceivably cut only a portion of the field at a time, thus spreading the drying process over days and even weeks, but this would present two problems. The first was that the hay would not be cut at optimum ripeness for highest nutritional value. The second was that the mown crop needed to be removed to allow room for the next crop to grow. While most farmers had barns for storing hay, they were large and ill suited to one-man haying operations, mainly because of their construction. Unless the barns had an elevated driveway or an aisle that allowed easy access to the haymow, the second-story mow would have to be filled by throwing hay up from the ground floor, making it often impossible to fill the mow completely.

Instead most barns had a system to fill the haymow from the top through a large opening at one end. In the peak of the barn, a carrier on a rail that ran the interior length of the barn would receive a fork load of hay lifted from the hay wagon by a rope attached to a horse that, on a signal, would pull the load up from the wagon. It would attach to the carrier and run into the barn along the rail. The man in the mow would signal when the load was where he wished it dropped, and the man on the hayrack would pull a trip rope, opening the fork to drop the hay. The worker in the mow then would distribute the hay evenly to the edges, building up the level until the fork loads could no longer enter the mow.

The minimum number of workers required in this operation was three: one to set the hayfork, another to arrange the hay in the mow, and a third to lead or ride the hay horse—this was likely to be a boy or girl since the work did not require great skill or judgment.

The draft horse commonly used for this role had a broad back that would not hold a saddle, so the job was done bareback. I began to ride the hay horse at the age of seven and continued into adolescence—not that I always displayed even the minimum amount of good judgment required. It was my habit to go barefoot in the summer in those years, and I failed to realize this recklessness on one occasion when I stood for a moment on the blind side of the old mare assigned to pull the hay into the barn. As she was stamping her feet to dislodge the omnipresent flies on her legs, she stepped heavily on my bare foot, and I could not get her to release her hoof. (The horses used for this haying task had to be quite strong; this one was a Belgian that weighed close to a ton.) My uncle, after hearing my screams, came to my rescue off the hay wagon with mixed irritation and amusement.

The two other workers had to be adults. They needed the strength to move the hay and set the fork as well as the judgment to do those tasks safely and efficiently. Even with care this was not always possible.

But stowing hay in the mow was not the only task. First, it had to be loaded on the hayrack in the field and taken to the barn. If one or two men loaded by hand, this was a slow process and took too much time to complete storing a crop of hay. A better way was to have a three-man crew and a mechanical hayloader. This method required one person to drive the horses pulling the wagon and two to distribute the hay on the wagon or hayrack. The mechanical hayloader, an implement attached to the rear of the hayrack, had arms with attached teeth that pulled the hay from a windrow, up high, above and over the back of the wagon. One person could not usually keep up with the stream of hay, so two were regarded as necessary to shape the load.

Again, the work required strength and judgment. It could be done with young adults, but not with boys. Riding a hayrack load of hay resembled sailing on a ship at sea with random motions, swaying from side to side, particularly if the field was filled with gopher or chipmunk holes and clods of dirt. The hay fields also contained hazards ranging from birds through bees. When mowing, I kept watching for flocks of quail that inhabited one of our fields. The birds were beautiful, and I had no desire to harm them. The same cannot be said for the bumblebees that lived in holes in the ground. They were a risk both in mowing and collecting the cured hay. Once, when my cousin Lyle was driving the tractor, pulling a hayloader and wagon with my father arranging the hay, he heard my father yell and jump off the hayrack. Bumblebees had come up the hayloader with the hay and had disrupted the process.

If keeping your footing on the hayrack was not treacherous enough, you also had to dodge your workmate's fork as he swung it around in preparation to move a bunch of hay. When I was in college, my uncle hired me and a one-eyed man who was an itinerant minister to load hay for a day while he drove a tractor pulling the hayrack and loader. The hired man was a frenetic worker who went after the hay with a vengeance, waving his fork wildly. Trying to keep my footing proved to be extremely tough; I feared being stabbed when I was on his blind side or falling off in an effort to avoid impalement.

Hay balers came later. The first were stationary machines; workers pitched hay into their hoppers to be compressed into rectangular bales tied with baling wire. Stationary gasoline engines furnished the power. With the advent of the small tractor, the baler became mobile. Instead of bringing the hay to the baler, the baler came to the hay.

Baling required that the hay be cured and in windrows, just as in putting up loose hay. The baler traveled around the field, spitting out bales as it went. The size of the bales varied according to the tension placed on the wires; the weight ranged from fifty to ninety pounds. The amount of tension depended upon the machine's operator; if he had been hired to bale, he usually followed the wishes of the landowner. Neither my father nor my uncles owned a baler, preferring to hire the work because they thought it was not economical to buy a machine that would be used only a few days a year.

The advantages of baled hay were in its compression. Loose hay is bulky and hard to transport, particularly on highways in wagons or trucks. Storing a sufficient amount for a winter required a large barn or the building of a haystack in the open, exposed to rain and snow. The stacks might become unstable and collapse if not carefully constructed or, as happened in one instance on our farm, when a few of our sheep ate into the bottom of the haystack deeply enough to cause the overhang to fall of its own weight, suffocating them. Loose hay is also harder to buy and sell because a hayload on a wagon may vary so greatly in size.

Hay bales, on the other hand, could be transported easily and, despite their weight variation, were at least quantifiable. While they were more difficult to place in a barn originally designed for loose hay, they took up less space. (They did, however, weigh more, and sometimes the weight proved too great for the haymow floor.) If stored outside, bales also stacked more easily and might be sheltered more readily by a tarp because of a more compact profile. In any case, they possessed still another advantage: when the bales were fed in winter, the slices of hay on the frozen ground had less wastage than loose hay easily trampled and scattered by the animals.

Not that bales were without headaches. The principal one was how to dispose of the used wires that had to be removed before the hay could be fed. Baling wire was ubiquitous in the 1930s, so common that it became a cliché to say that a machine was held together with that wire. But there was a limit to the amount that was needed for repairs. What to do with the rest? It cluttered up the barn and the feedlots, illustrating one of the less attractive features of rural living—the lack of recycling and other dumping facilities. The dealer who bought our wool also bought scrap metals, but baling wire lacked enough substance to be worth very much and was awkward to transport. It usually ended up instead in an unsightly pile along with tin cans, old tools, and other pieces of scrap in gullies or ditches, to help stay erosion.

New machines demanded new techniques. Putting up baled hay required more physical effort than putting up loose hay. At the start there were no mechanical loaders in the field for bales as there were for loose hay. This meant loading the bales on a hay wagon by hand, usually by grabbing the two wires binding the bale and lifting it onto the wagon while another worker stacked the bales uniformly. Unloading the bales reversed the process, unless the farm had an elevator. Sometimes a hay hook, similar in appearance and use to a longshoreman's, helped the laborer drag a bale into position. But it was still hard work.

Lifting bales onto a wagon all day might be considered equivalent to a number of repetitions in the gym, and with similar results. Any muscles I possess derive in part from this exercise, especially my work on Uncle Freeman's farm. I liked Uncle Freeman, but he was notoriously frugal. At the time the usual fee charged for baling was ten cents a bale, regardless of weight. At the beginning of haying, the operator would bale a few units to determine the size the owner wanted. Uncle Freeman would ask that the tension be increased, the result being a bale that weighed between ninety and a hundred pounds. If you lifted those all day, you had to develop muscles.

Baling hay has changed. Now bales are round and so heavy they must be lifted by a forklift or a front-end loader on a tractor. Their rise in popularity coincided with the demise of the barn. Because of their size and shape, round bales supposedly withstand rain and snow better than their rectangular predecessors and are more often seen outdoors, still in the field. Because of evolving equipment, the new bales require less storage space.

One technique that we used for a time proved, at least to us, short-lived. That was the hay cutter that minced the hay stems and leaves into small pieces. The theory behind its development seemed quite sound. It began with the readily observed phenomenon that animals preferred the leaves and smaller stems of hay and avoided the larger, more woody ones. The way to use all the hay, thought the designers of the cutter, was to harvest it in a way that mixed all the elements together so that all would be eaten. This would be done by cutting hay into very small bits. The essential equipment was a hay cutter that took hay from a windrow, chopped it into pieces, and blew it into a wagon. It was then carried to a barn where a blower blew the product into the barn or a stack.

The system was clearly derived from that used to make silage. But the designers neglected a crucial difference between silage and hay. Silage consisted of green plants, most often corn, cut green and put into a supposedly airtight silo to ferment. Hay, on the other hand, consisted of green plants cut green but then dried and put into a barn with the hope it would *not* ferment. This hope was not realized in this system.

In the first place, the determination of when the hay was properly cured proved much more difficult with this method. As a result, too green hay was not uncommon; blown into a barn it heated up and sometimes burst into flames that burned down the structure. A second, unforeseen hazard resulted from the fact that the chopped hay, even when not too green, weighed more than loose hay. The temptation to stuff the barn as full as possible sometimes led to the collapse of the mow floor.

We were fortunate to avoid either disaster, but we did have a stack of the chopped hay that gave us pause. It was a small stack, round, about ten feet in diameter, and almost ten feet high. It began to smoke after a week, and a small wisp continued to curl out of the stack for days afterward. Fortunately it never caught fire, though we found the innermost layer grey and ashen after the sheep had consumed the outer layer. The heat did not affect the palatability of the other layers as our sheep ate it greedily. I think it had fermented, or so it smelled. Perhaps it had become silage without the silo.

I was quite happy when the cut-hay experiment proved unworkable, because putting up hay with the chopper was extremely unpleasant. The process of chopping and blowing raised much dust and spread small particles of hay everywhere. While my cousin and I both wore goggles to protect our eyes when working with the chopped hay, we had no masks to cover our mouths and noses, such masks being uncommon at the time. After a day in the hay fields, I sneezed and coughed up black sputum for several days, and I am sure it affected my lungs.

Haying was a continuing job, but in early summer it took less time than cultivating corn. After the first cultivation, the one that paralleled the path of the planter, the cross cultivation was more arduous. Its path depended upon how well the planter had aligned the hills, and it had to cross the furrows and ridges thrown up by the first cultivation. When we first acquired a share, with some of my uncles, in a row-crop tractor, we ran it day and night trying to cultivate all the land we owned and rented. As a consequence the second cultivation, which should have proceeded slowly, had to be done more quickly. By this time I was old enough to take a shift relieving my father and allowing him to work elsewhere. It was quite an experience as the tractor bumped and jarred its way across the cornfield.

The third cultivation, again along the planting path, while bumpy was less so than the second. It still called for care on the part of the driver since the larger plants might have their roots cut or their tops broken by the cultivator frames. Speed still ruled, however.

By mid-July we had "laid by"—that is, finished the third cultivation of—the corn. But the fight against weeds in the pre-pesticide era continued. Now the weapon was the hoe, and locomotion came from the feet. In between days of haying or cutting and harvesting small grain, we walked the corn rows chopping out butterprint or smartweed in the high heat and humidity of mid-summer Iowa.

I believe the emphasis on maintaining a weed-free field was as much aesthetic as economic. Father scorned those farmers who allowed their fields to become weedy. (The velvet-leaf butterprint stood out clearly among soybeans, and the smartweed did as much in the oat fields.) He knew the little black seeds of the butterprint that entered the harvested crop would infect the fields the following year, but the truth was that most soybeans, like most corn, were from hybrids, so the current crop was not replanted.

Father's vendetta against weeds extended to fencerows as well. He wanted these trimmed so that passersby could see the fine crop, especially the rows facing US 63 that had cut parts of the farm into triangular fields. But this was not the sole reason; weed seeds could blow into the cropland. The best way to cut the weeds in the fencerows was by hand since they were too narrow or too heavily overgrown to accommodate even hand mowers. The tool used was the scythe, which had ancient roots and today serves as a symbol for death or Father Time. Swung properly, it was highly effective in felling weeds or grass. The trick was to find the proper rhythm, otherwise the swing became labored and backbreaking. I think I came close to that natural rhythm only a time or two.

I used to marvel at my father as he swung away ahead of me, cutting with ease and seemingly little effort. His clothes would be soaked in sweat, as was his old felt hat, and a residue of salt lay on parts of his shirt. Yet he worked at a pace I could not sustain.

There was little spare time in the summer; only sometimes did we celebrate the Fourth of July. I remember family picnics, but I do not remember parades or other patriotic exercises. Was it because we rarely went anywhere, or was it because those exercises did not exist in our area? My father often said he had only two holidays when growing up, the Fourth of July and Christmas. So the Fourth had some importance in his time.

If there were summer days when no chore seemed pressing, I could earn pocket money working for a neighbor. One
job that returned me to the cornfield was to detassel corn.
Corn plants reproduce by shedding pollen from the tassel
onto the silk of the ear. In other words, the plant is self-
pollinating. In order to create hybrid corn, the male element,
the pollen of one plant, must fertilize the female element of
another plant. The pollen, being light and wind-borne, can
easily fertilize other plants as long as they do not fertilize
themselves. The breeder prevented self-pollination by having the tassels of some plants removed, usually by rural
youths.

For every eight rows of corn, we worked to remove the
tassels from six. The tassels on the other two rows would then
pollinate the rest. The ears on those two rows were thus not
hybrid and were used as feed rather than sold as seed corn.

Tassels emerged at different times according to the season and the growth rate of each plant, so one sweep through
a cornfield was never enough to dispose of them all. Detassel-
ers had to cover the same ground several times until all tassels had been eliminated, regardless of weather conditions.
We did not work in the rain, but we did work immediately
after a rain when the field was muddy and the humidity
high, making for considerable discomfort. Insects frequently
damaged the corn leaves, leaving them even sharper.

In between haying and cutting weeds in July came
threshing. In our case the grain to be threshed was almost always oats. Planted in March, oats were the earliest small
grain to ripen. Wheat took longer, as did other crops such as
barley. The different growing seasons allowed for a longer
harvest period.

Until the late 1930s, harvesting oats involved two steps—
cutting and binding the grain into sheaves or bundles, then

threshing it by means of a separator. Later we hired a neighbor who owned a machine to combine the small amount of oats we raised. The combine, as the name suggests, combined the two operations into one.

Harvesting began when the grain was nearly ripe, as signaled by a change of color in the field from green to beige. But the oats could not be allowed to become too ripe since a strong wind or a heavy rain might then cause the heavy heads to collapse the stalks and bend them over, making harvesting quite difficult. The grain could ripen, like hay, after it was cut, provided the weather was not too cold or rainy. But it had to dry with the heads off the ground and the stalks in an upright position.

When McCormick invented his reaper in the mid-nineteenth century, it was a noted improvement over cutting the grain with a hand-swung cradle, a tool that resembled a scythe but had extensions to windrow the cut plants. Later improvements led to the binder, which not only cut the grain but also tied it into bundles. A mechanism that tied binder twine around a bunch of grain was the device that made the new machine such an improvement.

Either drawn by horses or by a tractor, the binder cut the grain in the same fashion as the haymower, by a cutter bar sliding over a fixed base with teeth. A reel consisting of about six wooden slats swept the grain over the cutting edge and onto a canvas bed, which then conveyed the grain to be gathered into a bunch, tied, and ejected. The entire procedure was controlled by an operator. In our case, when we had a tractor, the operator had no other responsibility as another person drove the tractor. If horses were used, the operator drove them and ran the binder.

The binder kicked out bundles at irregular intervals, though the operator tried to dump them as close to one another as possible on each pass around the standing grain. Perfect alignment could not be achieved because of the ever-shrinking size of the unmown patch as the binder did its work.

The shockers, one of which I became, gathered bundles into place in order to form a shock. I usually constructed a shock from nine bundles, starting with two placed against each other, followed by two more at ninety-degree angles, four added to the spaces in between, and one final bunch spread open to serve as a cap to shed rain. The procedure became automatic for me as shocks soon dotted the field. With three uncles helping, as was usually the case, a small field of oats could be cut and shocked in a day. The work was not difficult, and the setting was pleasant. I enjoyed it.

Threshing the grain happened later, giving the heads time for further drying in the shocks and also time for all owners in the group to cut and shock their grain. This usually meant that threshing occurred in August, depending, of course, on the time of initial planting.

The threshing ring, a truly neighborhood affair, became the important organization in the harvesting of small grains. The ring was a cooperative affair in which each participant owned one share, had one vote, and paid an equal amount for upkeep and necessary purchases. It had elected officers, minutes, and a common treasury. The ring might construct a shed to shelter the threshing machine on a member's land, and would usually rent the needed steam engine from a private owner (at least this was the arrangement in the ring to which my father belonged). Later, when tractors replaced the steam engine, the members often used their own tractors for power and would pay the chosen owner for the service.

The ring held regular meetings, annually or semi-annually. One meeting would be preparatory—its purpose was to get ready for the season. The work involved, first, the inspection and needed repair of the separator that took the head of the grain from the stalk. Members would grease the machine, check the belts, and make necessary adjustments.

The second task was to determine the schedule and route to be taken by the ring. Two major concerns shaped the plan of work: economy and equality. Each year threshing began at a different farm, allowing the members over the seasons an equal chance to begin. The advantage of an early start was that it usually meant better weather for the threshing. The longer the grain stood in shocks, the more likely that rain would spoil it and darken the straw, thus lowering the value of each.

The ring then plotted the route by building from the starting point. The basic principle was to make a circle that had the shortest circumference. Each year, then, a member might have a different place and time on the circle. While the equipment was portable, it traveled slowly (the steam engine in particular had a top speed of about three miles per hour). That feature plus the time required to set up and test-run the separator made a planned route necessary.

If the ring held semi-annual meetings, the second meeting occurred in the fall after the harvest. Then accounts were settled and members received income they had earned—for custom work, for example, such as threshing the grain for nonmembers.

Separators varied in size and in the power required to run them. Manufacturers measured their capacity in inches—the size of the threshing cylinder into which drivers pitched bundles of grain off their hay wagons. Once taken into the machine by a conveyor, the binder twine on the bundles was cut, allowing the individual stems of grain to travel over a series of shakers and screens that separated the stalk (straw) from the head. After the heads were blown by fans to separate the kernels from the chaff (outer hull, dust, and particles of straw), an auger fed the grain into a wagon. In some old photographs the grain is shown being funneled into sacks, presumably to be sold. In our threshing ring this never happened.

Power to run all these machines came from a pulley on the threshing machine connected with a crossed belt to another pulley on the steam engine or the tractor. The threshing, to be done efficiently, required considerable hands. One operator watched the tractor or steam engine; another did the same for the separator and also examined the grain as it emerged from the spout to determine its cleanliness. He also reexamined the straw to see if it contained too many grains being blown out and wasted.

Those two men operated only the threshing outfit; there were many more who fed it. Since bundles could be fed into the hopper from both sides simultaneously, a minimum of four hayracks were used, two unloading while two more were loading in the field. And in order to speed up loading, two men in the field pitched bundles to the hayracks. At the other end, at least two wagons had to be used to receive the newly threshed grain, one to be loaded while the other was unloaded. This demanded two more drivers. Finally, to speed up unloading, a "spike" scooper helped shovel the grain into a bin.

Thus the minimum number of workers necessary for the threshing operation was nine. This does not include the water boy who supplied water to thirsty workers, nor does it account for the times when additional hands were needed—for example, when the distance from field to threshing machine or from machine to grain bin was too long for drivers to maintain a steady flow of work. Nor does it count a worker who would build the straw into a stack. Straw could be blown into a pile on the ground, but if a stack had to be built, a man had to stand on top of the growing pile to arrange the straw into a well-shaped stack.

Straw presented no problem on the grain field in the binder/thresher process, as threshing removed it. With the combine, the straw ended up strewn over the next year's hay crop. This was not a problem if the stalks were short or thinly spread; they could remain on the field as fertilizer. But if they were long and thickly spread, they could choke out the crop they covered. In that case the straw had to be removed. Early in the 1930s this could be done by burning, as it was with cornstalks. Later, farmers baled their straw exactly as they baled their hay, using the same techniques. One reason for the shift was the increased value of the straw. Without a market for straw, there was no value in spending money to bale it.

Most farmers in the region used straw chiefly for animal bedding. Straw had little or no nutritional value; animals would eat it only if they had no alternative. Nor were other farmers likely to buy straw from their neighbors unless they had none of their own. A small market existed only for those who owned animals—recreational horsemen, commission merchants selling or buying sheep, hogs, or cattle, and others who did not farm.

Growing up, I performed most of the work roles in threshing with the exception of operating the machines or building the stack. I began carrying water, barefoot of course, when I was strong enough to manage the gallon pottery jugs, and graduated to pitching bundles onto hayracks in the field and spike scooping at the bin before being allowed to drive a team with a hayrack or a grain wagon.

I remember my scratched legs as I carried water in the fields and my aching back after scooping oats all day. I also remember the pride I took in driving Uncle Carl's team of matched greys with their fancier, better harness than ours and their more obedient and more easily managed work habits. (Uncle Carl kept his own team together for years, unlike ours which belonged to grandfather and which he would put together for only a short time.) I found satisfaction in all the work despite the drawbacks, the heat, the dirt, and the long hours.

Beyond the work itself, I enjoyed the break from the monotony of my routine and repetitive farm work, and the social aspects that expanded contacts beyond the family circle. This despite the inevitable teasing and tricks that always seemed part of the company of men—from hiding tools to questioning aspects of growing manhood.

A favorite game involved the use of tobacco. Few farmers smoked, at least not near flammable materials, but many used chewing tobacco, snuff, or "snoose" (no one called it smokeless tobacco in those days). My grandfather and three of my uncles all chewed tobacco. My uncle Carl also smoked both cigarettes and cigars, a fact he tried unsuccessfully to conceal from us.

The trick involved persuading the victim, usually young and naive, to try the chewing tobacco for the first time, then offering him water knowing that he would inadvertently swallow some of the tobacco juice if he drank. The juice would often induce vomiting or diarrhea in the victim, prompting great amusement among the tricksters.

Another more successful form of harassment was to question the masculinity of the younger boys and men by deriding their attempts to exhibit male characteristics—questioning the puniness of a faint mustache or the frequency of shaving or the absence of girlfriends. Like the tobacco stunt, it became stale after a while.

I also enjoyed the threshing ring for the food, both its quantity and quality. I knew, though, that the bountiful threshers' meal exacted a toll on the farmers' wives. It was often a matter of contention between my father and mother. He thought little about the cooking, I believe, while concentrating on the crop. She, on the other hand, worried about providing the meals. Just as farmers were judged on their tidy fields, their wives were judged on the excellence and abundance of their food. Several aspects of the threshing regime conspired to make my mother suspect that others had planned for her to do more than her fair share. The fact was, no one knew exactly what the schedule would be and hence could only approximate when the ring would arrive at a given farmstead.

Several conditions might affect the progress of the threshing. One was the state of the grain crop. Moisture such as a heavy dew could delay the morning start, or a light rain could end a day's work early. Another was the condition of the equipment: it was often old and subject to breakdowns requiring a time-consuming search for repair parts. These problems, along with others, often unforeseen, made arrival at a particular farm uncertain.

Still, one cannot help feeling sympathy for my mother when a threshing crew suddenly appeared at 10 a.m. She knew they would expect a big dinner in a few short hours, and she was unprepared. Before electrification we had no means of storing fresh meat. The nearest store was at Wright, a little crossroads two and a half miles down the road, and she never drove a car. My father, engrossed in getting ready for the threshing crew, would not take the time to go. (In any case, the store might not have meat as it stocked mostly canned goods and nonperishables.)

So my mother would have to scramble to prepare a dinner for twelve with what food was available. There would be vegetables in the garden, though by August the heat probably had pushed them beyond their earlier peak. She did have canned vegetables and ingredients to make the expected array of desserts. For meat she could go to the chicken house and select some roosters to kill, scald, pick, and fry.

She had help—my sisters and I, and sometimes a neighbor's wife; still, it was a hectic, anxious period of haste to prepare and serve the meal. And a 10 a.m. arrival meant there was no time at all to prepare the mid-morning lunch (10:30 a.m. or thereabouts) that threshers had come to expect. Nor was she able to persuade father to arrange for the crew to be taken to a restaurant in town. That too required time and advance notice.

I preferred to eat at home, though the one time father consented to take the threshing crew to a restaurant did provide a new experience for me. I had never before eaten in one. This one was an unexceptional older establishment in a less desirable part of town with a pressed-tin ceiling and forgettable food.

Mother's food was not forgettable. Like other wives on the threshing run, she aimed to provide a lavish meal with plenty of treats. We could always expect mashed potatoes with lots of butter, several kinds of desserts—usually pies—and lemonade or tea and coffee. She also made a great fried chicken that was usually the meat of choice for other families in the ring. Everyone ate heartily; it is difficult now even to imagine how much hungry men who are working hard can consume.

The men had eaten earlier. After a big breakfast, they had a mid-morning lunch that usually consisted of a sandwich, a piece of fruit, and a cookie, plus tea or lemonade.

After the midday dinner, threshers also expected to receive a mid-afternoon lunch (3:30 p.m.) that often duplicated the fare in mid-morning. Then they went home to do their chores and eat for a fifth time, supper. Breaks for snacks like these were not familiar to me during any other stint of work, and I found them quite agreeable.

The harvesting of small grains marked the coming end of the summer holiday for me as school was to resume after Labor Day. There was also a hiatus from work. The corn had been weeded, several times, and the barn was either full of hay or about to be filled with it. The corn harvest was still to come, probably in October.

Shocking oats: Uncle Carl drives an older, heavier non-row-crop tractor while Uncle Freeman mans what was originally a horse-drawn binder.

Respite: An In-Between Age

SOMETIME immediately after World War II, my grand-father remarked as we were on a family drive that if he were young and just starting out as a farmer, he would buy a team of horses and horse-powered equipment instead of a tractor and tractor-powered equipment. I believed then, and I do now, that he aimed these remarks at me. I had not yet decided about my future in farming.

The import of his remarks originated in his own experience. After all, this is how he had started more than sixty years earlier, and the immediate postwar period did resemble that following World War I. At that earlier time, convinced of the continuing prosperity of agriculture stimulated by wartime demand, farmers overextended themselves in buying land and found themselves burdened with debt. Impressed with the costs of buying a tractor and its related equipment, Grandfather would have chosen instead to invest a few hundred dollars for a pair of horses and used equipment.

He could find them easily enough. The number of draft animals in the United States peaked in 1918, at the same time Grandfather made the most money, and declined steadily through the 1920s and 1930s as tractors replaced them. By the 1940s tractors were quite cheap in relative terms. Farmers sold off their draft animals, keeping some for light chores around the farm or continuing to breed them for show or for sentimental reasons. The demand for draft animals created by their destruction in Europe in World War I had ended, and the worldwide depression of the thirties would have limited overseas purchases even if there had been a demand. In the United States horses were often sought by those who raised mink and other small animals and bought horse meat to feed them.

A phenomenon of the times while I was growing up were slaughterhouses that specialized in horse butchering. These were not uncommon. As I went with truckloads of market animals to livestock terminals, I would see a building where horses were slaughtered. No one in the area seemed to want to talk about horse meat, probably because the subject was taboo, but rumors persisted that the meat from the facility appeared on the tables of the little cafés next to the livestock terminals, under the guise of beef. We usually ate in such a café before returning home, and I sometimes wondered if it was my imagination, or was the meat redder and sweeter?

Used horse-drawn equipment was also easy to come by. At almost any farm or auction barn one could buy a riding plow or corn cultivator or drill at a cheap price. (I knew because I went to many such sales; my retired grandfather amused himself by attending both farm sales and auction barns, and he sometimes took me.) Most farms also owned machinery that could be used either with a tractor or horses—harrows, hay wagons, manure spreaders—by making adjustments; and some had equipment reserved for use only with horses. We had both.

The transition to tractor power proceeded relatively slowly. The first and most obvious problem for farmers was a lack of capital to purchase the new equipment and replace all the old. The second was the fact that most farmsteads such as ours were ill-equipped to make the transition. They had too many buildings that had lost their purpose; they had fields that were poorly shaped or too small for the most effective use of tractors. All this is apparent in a comparison of a farmyard of the 1930s with today's counterpart. The one I knew growing up consisted of several large barns, a corncrib, two smaller outbuildings for small grains such as oats or wheat, and, of course, a hog house, a brooder house, and a henhouse. Many Midwestern farms today, having dispensed with livestock altogether, no longer need buildings to house animals or even barns to store hay. Their farmyard consists of a machine shed, usually a pole building with metal sheeting. If the modern farm specializes in raising or feeding animals, there need be only buildings that house a particular kind of animal. There are fewer buildings scattered around.

Acquiring a tractor could relieve the farmer of problems caused by horses, particularly those that Grandfather loaned to us while continuing to train them to work the fields. They smashed fences and gates and tore up equipment in their flight and fear. I recall one incident with a dramatic scenario. After arriving home one summer night and going to bed, I was roused from a deep sleep sometime after midnight by the dreaded message that dogs were in our sheep. So I got up, put on a pair of overalls over my pajamas, got my gun, an old .22 rifle, and set off with my father to assess the situation.

During those hard times, feral dogs posed a real threat to farm animals. Most of these dogs had been released in the country by owners who no longer wanted or could afford them. They ran in packs that hunted together and preyed on domestic animals for food. The dogs found chickens an easy target when they ranged freely during the day but found them more difficult to catch at night when they returned to sleep inside the chicken house. With sheep that remained outside almost all the time, it was a different matter. At night, sheep were vulnerable, and dogs could and did wreak havoc on them. The pack would kill some and injure more in what seemed to be an urge to wanton destruction. They tore open gaping wounds that became easily infected and resulted in considerable suffering for the sheep, if not death. Because of this havoc and because the sheep provided some of our livelihood, I would not hesitate to shoot these wild creatures even though I loved animals, especially dogs.

That night we found no dogs, though they had attacked the sheep herd and wounded some of them. Meanwhile, our voices and the light of our flashlights frightened the horses, who smashed several gates in their panic. Father got out the car to round them up, but he instructed me to remain at the crossroads by our farm to turn the animals back into the barnyard when they returned. By that time the night was quite cool, and I was soaking wet to above my knees because of the heavy dew. Cold and feeling put upon, I reacted badly when a passing motorist stopped. I don't know his motive since I spoke first, asking him what he wanted in what must have seemed a threatening manner. I think he then spotted my rifle, for he sped away as if he were in a drag race. I got some satisfaction from the incident, but not enough to affect the work I knew was in the offing in repairing the damage to the gates and in treating the dog-bitten sheep.

Besides the problems presented by horses, the equipment required in using them was old and needed repair or replacement. This was a result of ordinary wear and tear but also of the unusual weather conditions of the 1930s. The drought of those depression years shrank wooden sections of horse-drawn implements and baked the soil so hard that cultivation was difficult. The harness that enabled our team to pull various pieces of equipment had become quite rotten and subject to breaks. I cannot remember the many times my father got out his box of copper rivets, an old iron, a punch, and a hammer to repair a broken piece of leather. He grew remarkably skilled at riveting ends together to make the leather harness workable again. Lack of money prevented him from buying new harnesses. Even if he had had it, the question was whether it would be better spent on a tractor or new tractor-specific implements.

Lack of capital was one of the disadvantages of switching to tractors. It was not the original cost of the tractor alone that strained farmers' resources. While some horse-drawn implements could be converted for use with tractors, others such as plows could not. Thus buying a tractor often called for the purchase of additional implements as well. Almost no farmer could raise that much capital at the time. Instead most tractor owners struggled to get by with awkward, leftover equipment.

Tractors also required continuing expenditures. The farmer had to purchase gas at regular intervals as well as oil and grease. He had to replace batteries and tires. While early tractors were simple, they were not as simple as the horses they replaced. Repairs often required the visits of mechanics from dealers, and were expensive. Baling wire, the traditional solution to many problems, no longer served.

This need for a continual source of money to pay for necessary power in the field changed the balance of the agricultural equation. More and more of the emphasis in farming was to have a larger cash crop—and thus more cropland—to pay for those expanded necessities the farmer could not raise.

Another difficulty with tractors came from the physical shape of farm fields, the fences on small plots, and buildings not suitable for a new kind of agriculture.

Fences of any kind were a problem for the efficient use of tractor power. The most difficult areas to plow, cultivate, and harvest were those nearest the fence line because of the space needed to turn around the tractor. In using horses for cultivation, the skilled driver could maneuver his team in such a way as to trample down little of his crop in the process of reversing direction. It was less easy to do this with a tractor, which was heavier, went faster, and was often operated with less skill. Consequently these rows of corn cultivated with a row-crop tractor frequently had plants missing at every fencerow where the tractor operator turned.

Fencerows were not the most vexing problem for tractor use; it was the fences themselves. These divided farmland into small segments that did not allow full utilization of the tractor's potential. If your largest field was just twenty-six acres, as ours was, and the smallest was thirteen, you lost much time going from one field to the next, or turning at the ends of the field instead of going straight on longer rows. It became obvious that the best way to utilize the tractor was to sell the livestock and tear out the fences. This did not mean the end of separate fields. Farmers could grow different crops in different sections, but without fences as dividers.

Without livestock, farms offered a different way of life. There were fewer or no chores. The animals did not have to be fed or milked; their manure did not have to be hauled away. Their health did not have to be monitored and their offspring raised. There would be no need to make hay or harvest oats. Work would not be done daily but would instead be intensive only at planting and harvest time.

There was a cost, however. While there was more land available for the cash crop, there would be no animal manure to maintain soil fertility. An alternative had to be found in chemical fertilizers. So part of the return from the added acreage went for fertilizer. And part of it went to buy the food that was no longer raised on the farm—milk, eggs, and meat.

When I was growing up, no farmer I knew bought milk or eggs or meat, but by the 1940s this became more common. Not that it happened all at once. More often a farmer phased out one kind of animal while retaining others. He might give up milking a few cows or raising a few chickens while holding on to a few hogs or cattle for meat.

Most boys welcomed the end of having to milk cows, an unpleasant chore particularly in winter when cows had chapped teats and often kicked when they felt the cold fingers of the milker. Other chores brought fewer demands and could be done at less regular hours. Hogs and chickens ate out of feeders that needed only to be kept full, a job that could be done at 10 a.m. instead of 5 a.m. Family members might be less confined in their social life as they did not have to rush home at milking time. On the other hand, in these changes farmers' wives lost control of the butter and egg money and had to make other arrangements for household and personal expenses.

In other words, the shift to a different kind of agriculture signaled a change in ways of life that brought farm families closer to living like their neighbors in town.

Before this shift in spending patterns, the country store had an advantage in attracting rural shoppers. The owner would trade necessities to the farmer in return for milk and eggs. He rarely stocked perishables such as fresh meat or vegetables, and he usually extended credit to his customers. In our case, Earl Witt's store at Wright, a crossroads store, provided these services along with a post office, dry goods, and school textbooks. But Witt lost out in the later 1930s to the A&P in Oskaloosa that featured a greater variety of fresh produce, to JCPenney and Sears, Roebuck for clothes, and to the Mahaska Book Store for books. We shopped only once a week because we now had electricity to power a refrigerator where we could store our perishable items, just like people in town. A fitting conclusion to Witt's store came when he left Wright and had his house moved to Oskaloosa.

The shape of the fields was of little consequence for a general-purpose farm but of great importance for a specialized operation. The same was true for the buildings on the land.

Our main barn had little potential for conversion to a different farming pattern. The raised floor was uneven because freezing and thawing had shifted the rocks and sections of the barn in different directions. It could not support the extra weight that tractor or tractor-driven machinery would place on it even if they could have been driven into the barn, which they could not. The floor of the haymow provided a low ceiling that would not accommodate anything very tall on the ground floor, and the mow itself had little use except to store vast quantities of hay that would not be needed if there were no animals to feed. The holding shed at the far end had the same low ceiling and also had two wooden support posts in the middle that made maneuvering inside it difficult. Along with the hay mangers, the posts limited the use of space by dividing the shed into smaller areas—not an obstacle to cows but certainly to machines.

Few alternatives to the barn's patterns of usage seemed available. One of them was a conversion made by Uncle Frank when he bought Grandfather's farm after his death. He jacked up the barn and put a concrete foundation with a floor under it. He then used the barn for a confinement hog operation, with heaters, steel pens, and piped-in water. This worked as a viable hog operation despite the heat loss in the high roof in the winter.

Our second barn was even less suited to conversion. It had a dirt floor and leaned even more as it moved from its stone piles. It also had a lower ceiling on the ground level. (Once, when the hay horse I was riding became frightened at a piece of paper, it ran into the barn, and had I not ducked I would have been knocked off.)

Our barns gradually fell into disuse as we needed fewer horses or cows, and today the structures have vanished altogether. When I see the old homestead, I wonder what became of them. Are they decorating the wall of a rec room somewhere, or have they become part of a Yankee barn? Or were they simply burned to the ground?

Neither the fields' shapes nor the barns' structure led to the efficient use of tractor power. But changing them was not the first priority. The immediate goal was to get together enough money to make use of the new source of power, but that seemed impossible in a time of depression.

A complete makeover would have been ideal. This would have entailed tearing out most or all of the fences, razing both barns and other outbuildings, and moving to an all-crop operation. Another possibility to save labor and expense was to shift to another kind of animal operation, to stop feeding lambs. The introduction of electricity created still other possibilities. One was a commercial dairy operation; the other was a chicken or hog confinement system.

Electricity allowed a farmer to milk many more cows than he could by hand. On our general-purpose farm my father and I could milk a maximum of five cows (he did three and I did two). With electric milkers, the limits would be placed only by the facilities—barn space, pasture acreage, and so forth. New structures would have to be built. These

might include silos to contain the silage that was an important part of dairy cattle diet, plus a remodeling of the barn
to provide more room for a milking parlor and its equipment.
The milking parlor would include stanchions for the cows
and a system of pipes to carry the milk to a storage tank. It
would need both plumbing and electrical work.

A dairy operation in the age of electricity also had to con-
form to new and higher sanitation standards, which could be
achieved only with considerably more equipment. The milk
we took from our few cows fed us and some of our animals.
The separated cream went into a ten-gallon can where it
stood unrefrigerated for a week before being sold to a local
creamery. In the summer it became very sour indeed, so sour
that I wondered how it could be turned into decent-tasting
butter and ice cream.

The quantity of milk from a larger herd of dairy cattle
would require a refrigerated tank to hold the milk until
picked up and, for best results, a pipe system to deliver the
milk from cow to tank. It would also require a hot-water
heater to provide water for washing the cows' udders and for
sanitizing the entire system.

But that was not all. To build a dairy herd, even a small
one, required both time and capital. A good-quality herd
might require several generations of cows to produce a profitable operation.

Raising pigs and chickens in confinement required less
elaborate structural changes but had other unique disadvantages. The practice had just begun and in the case of the hog
operation had not yet developed a market that could handle
large numbers. Too, the new commercial farms that specialized in raising germ-free pigs were not well accepted. With
both poultry and hogs, confinement multiplied disease and
injury. The early methods were chancy. Large packers con-

tracted with farmers to feed out animals to company specifications, and supplied the necessary capital. But farmers were unwilling to become hired hands on their own land.

Above all, capital was in short supply. Banks hesitated to loan money to farmers, for good reason given the spate of bankruptcies and the abandonment of farms during the Great Depression. New Deal programs to help fill the need for farm credit never provided enough money. Even if they had, my father and his brothers, good Republicans, were in principle opposed to such attempts. My father especially would not willingly assume much more debt, obsessed as he was with paying off the land loan owed to my great-uncle Morris.

The only option seemed to be to begin changing to a modern, tractor-powered farm with as little investment as possible while retaining many of the elements of an older farming tradition. It was an in-between age.

The change was gradual, more of a shift in kinds of tractors than from horsepower to tractor power. Before World War I, large, clumsy tractors had begun to appear on Midwestern farms. But the major work of cultivating row crops such as corn and soybeans, in an era before the widespread use of herbicides and insecticides, still rested on horses.

The antique tractors did expand the amount of cropland that one family could cultivate. And along with the cheap automobiles of the time, they provided laboratories in educating a generation of farmers into the basics of machine operation and maintenance. By the 1920s all of my extended family, my father and my uncles, had married and owned cars. They also had experience with tractors used to power the threshing machine and for other chores apart from row crops. All had some fundamental mechanical knowledge. Uncle Dick, in particular, had a reputation for being a good backyard mechanic. My father knew more than his two younger brothers but probably less than the next two older ones.

By the late 1930s all were ready to move in a new direction. Consequently four of them—my father and Uncles Freeman, Carl, and Dick—pooled their resources and bought a new Case row-crop tractor which they used to cultivate all their farms plus another rented four-hundred-acre section of land. They did this by running the tractor day and night, taking turns at the wheel, during the seasons. I never knew why Uncle Frank was not in the pool, but I suspect it was owing to his greater physical and social isolation from the rest of the family, living three miles from our farm. An individual of strong opinions and not reluctant to express them, he probably would not have fit well in such a cooperative venture.

The age of the 1920s and 1930s saw the great growth of both tractor manufacturers and the sales of gasoline-powered tractors. World War I greatly expanded the use of tractors as the high demand for horses overseas made them scarcer, and as farm prices rose, farmers were able to buy tractors. In 1910 there were only about a thousand gasoline-powered tractors in existence; by 1920 manufacturers had sold 250,000, and by 1930 almost a million were available for farm use. Not all were row-crop models. Many versions were built to meet the needs of different kinds of farms.

Ford had the lead in the 1920s with his Fordson tractor, just as he had led the car market with his Model T. His tractor was introduced during World War I to replace horses, but it soon had competitors. All shared similar characteristics. They were lightweight and, by today's standards, underpowered. Our Case, for example, had a rating of about thirty horsepower. They were fast: one tractor manufacturer advertised a road speed of sixty miles per hour, enabling farmers to travel quickly from field to field or farm to farm. Their main advantage, though, was that they could cultivate row crops. This became possible because of the spacing of the wheels that enabled the tractor to straddle crop rows, the placement of cultivator shovels to plow between the rows, and the light weight that did not excessively pack the ground.

The technological changes that made this possible included replacing iron-lugged wheels with rubber tires, making back wheels that could be adjusted to accommodate different width rows, and providing a hydraulic mechanism to raise and lower the cultivators. These tractors retained the side pulley for belt work and had a power takeoff at the rear that operated pull-type equipment such as mowers and corn pickers.

The Fordson was a four-wheel machine with the wheels at the four corners, but this was not the form most row-crop tractors took. Most of the popular models where I grew up had two large back wheels and two wheels or one smaller one located in the middle of the front end. The front-wheel placement reflected two approaches to the problem of navigating crop rows. The Fordson tractor allowed the wheels to straddle two rows while the more popular solution allowed the front wheel to go between two rows. Our tractors were of the second type and had several advantages. They were taller, permitting greater visibility for the driver and greater clearance for the new crop, especially the corn plants. These could easily break if they were too tall when the field was "laid by," usually on its third cultivation. On the other hand, these tractors were not as stable when pulling a heavy load because of the weight distribution. In extreme circumstances the front end would rear up as the machine strained to pull forward.

By the 1930s many manufacturers competed to build tractors. Their names reflected a variety of origins. Minneapolis-Moline carried the names of two cities while Allis-Chalmers were built in West Allis, a suburb of Milwaukee. Massey-Ferguson was an amalgam of two family names, the first a famous Canadian one. McCormick-Deering celebrated the inventor of the first successful reaper just as John Deere memorialized the inventor of the steel plow.

Like the automobile, the age of the tractor coincided with the rise of advertising in the 1920s. Tractor manufacturers spent considerable money to promote their products. Allis-Chalmers, for example, sponsored the famed race-car driver Barney Oldfield when he raced the company's tractors at fairs and other rural events. At each manufacturer's allotted space on machinery row at local and state fairs, salesmen handed out inexpensive gifts as well as free literature to prospective buyers and their male children.

As a result, all boys my age knew a great deal about the major makers of farm machinery and could discuss their strengths and weaknesses with authority. They could identify the manufacturer by the tractor's color since each maker chose a particular hue for its product. Case, our favorite brand, was Chinese red, or grey and red; Farmall, made by International Harvester, was bright red; Allis-Chalmers was pumpkin orange; John Deere was bright green with a yellow deer; Oliver was olive green; and Fordson was plain grey. We all could identify the pop-pop-pop of John Deere's two-cycle engine even if the tractor was nowhere in sight.

Our Case tractor seemed an anomaly in a sea of orange, for our neighbors had Allis-Chalmers. But we escaped the connection that my peers made between farming success and the kind of tractor we drove because they recognized that my father was an excellent farmer. The poorest farmer in the immediate region had a John Deere that he drove very badly (he never learned to drive a car), so that implement line earned the boys' scorn. "Popping John" (the John Deere) became an object of derision for us. Who could have guessed the brand would become the dominant machine in the country?

Neighbor boys, like me, wanted to drive the new machines as their families bought them, and they, like me, did so by ages ten to fifteen with only a few minor accidents. Parental permission to climb into the tractor seat usually followed from the early recognition that young help was necessary and that many tasks required more than one worker. When the farm implements used with the tractor were leftovers from horse-drawn days, the adjustments in the operation were made from the driver's seat on the machine, not on the tractor. With a horse-drawn mower, for example, the driver raised and lowered the cutter bar mechanically by hand from his seat. But if the mower was pulled by a tractor, the tractor driver could not operate the bar. Another person had to do it from the mower's seat.

Not that driving a tractor of that era was simple. Most did not come equipped with an electric starter, so they had to be cranked. The John Deere had a unique system: you started it by twisting a wheel on the side of the engine. Nor were the controls familiar. The Case had a hand clutch located at the right of the steering wheel and a hand throttle on the steering post. A foot brake for each side was at the driver's feet. The floor-mounted gearshift was in the middle, under the steering wheel.

In more complex maneuvers, the manipulation of these controls was extremely difficult. In reversing directions to return across a cornfield, care had to be taken not to uproot a great number of plants. Here were the required steps when

cultivating corn: As the end of the row approached, the
driver had to first slow the tractor, then raise the cultivator
shovels at the moment the row ended while simultaneously
standing on the brake pedal on the side to which he was turning. At the same time he had to steer to avoid running over
plants. He then released the brake to avoid oversteering and
turned the front wheels into the proper row while lowering
the shovels to engage and speeding up to make another pass
through the field. This was not an easy move for an adult, let
alone an eleven-year-old boy weighing a hundred pounds.
Proof of the difficulty lay in the missing plants that gave end
rows an irregular look, like the missing teeth in a Halloween
jack-o'-lantern.

Beyond the difficult maneuvers, driving a tractor involved a general discomfort. Early tractors lacked cabs, so
their seats were open to the elements. In summer the sun
burned the driver as dust clogged his nose; in winter the
driver froze his fingers and toes as the wind blew snow and
sleet in his face. (Uncle Freeman purchased a canvas shield
that diverted some engine heat toward the driver, but we
never had one.) Tractor seats resembled other implement
seats: they lacked hydraulic cylinders to smooth out bumps
and jars, relying on springs instead. Given the uneven surface of most fields, this guaranteed a rough ride, especially
during cross-cultivation, which was performed at considerable speed because of the large area to be covered.

I suffered no permanent back damage from the jolting
ride, as Uncle Freeman did. Thrown from a horse when
young, he further injured his back on rough-riding tractors.
He finally sold his farm and, after a stay in New Mexico,
moved back to southern Iowa to graze cattle, a practice that
required less tractor riding. My own experience did not leave

me unaffected. After a day's riding the bucking tractor, I still felt the motion in bed until I fell asleep.

The major adjustment called for in a transitional age was the greater room required in turning with mixed equipment. The horse-drawn equipment had tongues long enough to accommodate a horse on either side, but adding a tractor to the end of the tongue increased the length of the entire rig by the tractor's length. This changed one's calculations for making turns in cutting hay, pulling a binder, going around a barn corner, and other similar tasks.

The greater length could have been eliminated by buying new equipment with shorter tongues specifically designed for tractor use. But there was little money for such a purchase, and besides, wagons and hayracks still could be used with both horses and tractors. Sometimes we used a tractor to pull a hayrack, but other times we used the horses. The switch often depended on the season. In the summer, in the midst of putting up hay, we used the tractor because we had full days of work and the tractor never tired. In the winter, when we wanted to feed hay to our sheep, it was both easier and more economical to hitch up the horses instead of starting up the tractor. And the horses needed the exercise to throw off some of their excess energy.

Remember too that one set of running gears often served as the wheels for both wagons and hayracks. The wagon box would be lifted off and placed on sawhorses or planks, to be replaced by a hayrack that had been waiting its turn during haying season. With a shorter tongue, neither wagon nor hayrack could be horse-driven.

Still older wagons lingered in farmyards, relics from an earlier age. My grandfather had a Studebaker wagon left over from the Civil War era that gradually rotted away while standing in his barnyard. We also had a model from an earlier era, but like his, it had lost most of its utility and was rarely used.

The older wagons had features missing from more modern versions. They had brakes in the form of a wooden block operated by an iron lever at the driver's right hand. The driver sat on a removable wooden bench seat with an iron leaf spring on either end. (The whole setup can still be seen in the stagecoaches and spring wagons of Western movies.) If you had no load, or a light load, you could have a pleasant and easy ride in the wagon since you could sit down and enjoy the view.

But certain features limited the older wagon's usefulness. The high wheels designed to go through both water and mud allowed less room for a wagon box or hayrack, and there was little need for a brake in everyday farm use. A bigger problem was the wood used in construction. The high wheels were all wood except for an iron strip around the circumference. When the wood shrank, the iron tire was loosened and so were the spokes. Age, aided by the elements, rendered all the wooden parts more fragile. Drought conditions in the 1930s didn't help. Pulling an old wagon with a tractor over bumpy terrain could often break parts or throw off an iron tire. I myself broke at least one undercarriage in executing a right-angle turn with a hayrack going around a barn corner.

Newer wagons fixed some of these problems. The running gears had smaller iron wheels and less wood in their construction. They could be pulled faster, particularly over hard-surfaced roads, though they made a large racket in the process, but nonetheless were better suited to being drawn by horses.

All horse-drawn equipment needed to be fitted with rubber pneumatic tires in order to be adequate for use with tractors. They needed to be phased out altogether as newer pieces became available that were specifically designed for tractor use.

I knew that time was coming when we bought a set of running gears with rubber tires, and then I understood why my father never bought a new set of harnesses even after World War II when he had the money to pay for it. Far better to rivet the broken sides of the leather straps and save the money for a hydraulic piston to reduce the impact of the bouncing tractor seat.

AUTUMN

Husking corn: the husker tosses an ear in the direction of the wagon.
The team is trained to move and stop on oral commands.

AUTUMN was the season of harvest. It was also the season with the most memorable views and smells. The soft maple trees that bordered our yard showered down their yellow and red leaves instead of the green branches shed in the storms of spring and summer. No fire restriction prevented us from raking them up and burning them; the smoke remains in my olfactory memory and evokes once again a time and place.

The smoke from burning leaves joined with that from fields of burning cornstalks, for in my earliest years farmers cleared their fields for the next year's crops in this fashion. The broken stalks would be arranged in piles or more often in rows and burned. My memory is of many fires at night as we burned our dead stalks at the same time our neighbors did theirs. It was a magic moment as the ring of fire seemed to surround all of us.

Fire fascinated me, and there was enough of it around to satisfy that fascination. Like most other farmers, we had a site dedicated to burning trash. It was a pile of fine grey ash over a circle of scorched earth on the border of our woodlot. Here we piled fallen tree branches, cardboard cartons, paper, and other combustibles to be burned at irregular intervals. I enjoyed setting the pile afire and once did it inadvertently before my father wanted me to do so. Although he was not physically abusive, he did believe in spanking, and the one he gave me on that occasion was one to remember.

Fires were greatly to be feared in those days when our farms were without the benefit of a county fire department. If a house or barn caught on fire, usually it was destroyed; there was no piped water or powered pressure systems. My grandfather's house burned down in 1934. Luckily he and my grandmother survived, but the neighboring Pringles and their niece and nephew later died in a house fire. Despite these examples and the fear they engendered, farmers, and we ourselves, were careless in setting fires. Sometimes our cornstalk fires got away from us and threatened others' fields. They were more dangerous than we imagined.

Another pleasant memory remains of those autumns on the farm. Our small woodlot contained a number of black walnut trees that shed their nuts in the fall. We harvested the large round and green nuts we found on the ground. It was usually Indian Summer with mild sunny weather, a perfect time to roam. We stripped the green outer coverings of the walnuts by putting them in a hand-cranked corn sheller or by hammering them on a hard surface. Although we tried hard to avoid stains, our hands usually turned brown from the outer hulls of the walnuts. Then we ate these strong- and distinctive-flavored nuts the rest of the year in cookies and cakes.

But the harvest occurred before the destruction of the cornstalks. In the days before we had a mechanical corn picker, picking the corn by hand ensured a long harvest season. A skilled husker could pick a hundred bushels a day— but he would have to be a young man who was not burdened with many other responsibilities. On a hundred-acre farm such as ours, which had good crop yields of eighty to one hundred bushels per acre, with at least half the acreage in corn, it would take one man the better part of two months to pick all the crop. (Remember, we never worked on Sunday, nor did our neighbors. Going to town on Saturday might mean a loss of half a day or evening from work; and wet weather would halt work until the muddy fields had dried.)

I never became a good cornhusker; indeed I was a miserable failure in that role. The process was simple. The husker wore cotton gloves and had a hook or peg on one hand. These were triangular metal fitted into a leather piece that covered the palm or thumb. He grasped the ear with the other hand while he stripped away the cornhusks with the hook or peg. He then snapped the ear from the stalk and threw it into the accompanying wagon, using the backboard or bangboard located on one side to bank it in. A good husker would strip most of the shucks off the ear in several quick moves, but he could not take the time to make sure that all were gone. Consequently the corn in the wagon often had a tattered look, with pieces of husks clinging to half-exposed ears.

My first attempt at husking revealed how slow I was. My father sent me out to the field one Saturday morning with a team and wagon with orders to pick a full load. It was early in the fall, and the corn was still too immature to crib. We had finished feeding the old corn from the preceding year's crop and needed more grain to feed the hungry livestock.

None of the corn in the field had been harvested; the field had not yet been, in the parlance of the time, "opened up." Since we had planted the corn to the field's edge with only a narrow grassy fence row of two to three feet, there was no way to begin picking except to drive the team and wagon into the field so as to knock down two rows of unharvested corn.

Opening up a field was slow work. The husker had to stoop over to pick the corn from the fallen stalks, husk it, and throw it into the wagon's narrow back without benefit of the backboard. Then he had to pick ears from the adjoining two rows as well.

I moved slowly down the cornfield, further delayed by my desire to shuck the corn as cleanly as possible. It took me all morning and some of the afternoon to collect less than a full load. So delayed was I that my mother feared I had suffered an accident. By happenstance my grandfather came by to visit, so she sent him to the field to find me. He did and told me to stop work and go eat the delayed dinner my mother had prepared.

By the time I had matured enough to learn the technique and master the necessary rhythm to be a halfway decent cornhusker, we owned a tractor and a mechanical cornpicker. My father believed, correctly, that they were too dangerous for me to operate, so he consigned me to driving the wagon that the picker filled with corn.

The early cornpicking machines were separate units connected by a takeoff that provided the power to operate the picker through a rectangular rotating bar at the rear of the tractor. The power takeoff enabled the chain drives in the two noses of the cornpicker to pull the stalks into the machine as it progressed down the field. This is where the danger lay.

Cornpickers, like mowers, had a tendency to clog, either with clumps of dirt or with a bunch of cornstalks. In that event the tractor driver had to stop and manually unclog the picker. The easiest way, if you were in a hurry—and most farmers were always in a hurry—was to stop the tractor but not the power takeoff. Unclogging was easier if the chains could help pull out the obstruction. But that was not the safe way. The power takeoff might catch part of the operator's clothing. By the time of corn harvest, it was chilly enough in Iowa that farmers usually wore several layers of clothing. Once caught by the bar, the farmer's clothes would wrap up, his legs might break, or he might suffer serious injury while trapped in the field.

This almost happened to my father. One day as he stepped down off the tractor, the power takeoff caught his overalls and tore off his pant leg, his long winter underwear, and his rubber overshoe. He was not seriously injured, probably because his clothing was old and tore more easily than new, tougher denim.

More serious was getting caught in the snapping rolls of the cornpicker. The limb involved was usually an arm or at least a hand trapped as a clog suddenly released and the gathering chains began pulling the operator into the rolls. He had little chance of releasing himself save by heroic measures such as self-amputation or by waiting for someone to discover his plight. With the advent of the cornpicker came also the not uncommon sight of a farmer with an artificial hand or arm.

Much of the time I was growing up, my father used still another method to harvest our corn crop. He believed, in common with today's organic farmers, that the best way to market the corn was through livestock that would eat the grain and then in turn be eaten themselves. The manure they left behind would fertilize the soil and help compensate for the fertility taken from it by the crop.

Unlike most of the farms that surrounded us, our efforts in the autumn harvest season primarily involved animals. We did not have to pick much corn by hand or by picker because we needed only enough to feed our horses, cows, and laying hens for the coming winter. Our hay crop was in the barn, all three clover cuttings. The oats bin had long ago been filled.

By the beginning of autumn we had also harvested the food to carry the family through the winter. Most of the last vegetables from our garden had been picked, some, such as green tomatoes, even before ripening. Root crops were in the cellar, and the remaining roosters, those we had not eaten, had been sold to a local produce agent. We had also sold the pigs we raised or purchased in the spring while reserving several for our own use.

Fall was the season for planning the next year's animal crops, at least some of them. Our mares and cows had been bred in the summer because of their longer gestation periods. But it was time to turn the ram in with the ewes and the boar in with the sows. This would require more bookkeeping in order to predict the probable birthdates of next season's lambs and pigs, and closer observation of the sheep flock and hog herd to determine when each female was bred. Unlike the cows and mares, when impregnation time was known because the male animals had to be kept segregated until the female showed signs of being ready for breeding, the ewes and sows were too numerous to breed individually.

Our main attention, however, was focused elsewhere—upon our cash crop, which was our animals. While we earned a little income from the pigs and sheep we raised, the great bulk came from the feeder livestock we bought in the fall and sold in the winter. Hence our main task was to keep the animals alive and well, seeing they had adequate food to supplement the corn, salt and other minerals, and water. This called for constant inspection of the animals to determine their growth and fitness, feed them hay to provide the requisite fiber that ruminants (cows and sheep) require, and pump the water by hand to satisfy a continuous thirst, and select out those that were ill. Consequently when I labored pumping water for two hours on a warm October day, I could see a neighboring farmer picking his corn. His was a more common autumn work, but mine was no less seasonal.

The feeder livestock that my father and three of his four brothers chose for a cash crop were sheep. It was a family tradition, and feeding sheep had several advantages for a small farmer with little capital. One was rapid turnover: lambs purchased in September would be large and fat enough to be sold in late November or early December for the holiday markets. There was less risk of market price changes for lamb in three months of feeding than in the eighteen months required to finish off feeder calves from time of purchase to time of sale. There was also less need for pasture land or hay than with calves because sheep were purchased before the cold weather required more hay, or after the warm weather when extensive grass was necessary.

I never quite understood why we bought our feeder lambs, cattle, or pigs instead of raising them ourselves. Part of it, again, was custom and family tradition. But also, our farm lacked the necessary facilities for larger-scale livestock breeding and birthing. We could raise a few lambs and calves since they could be born outside or in the barns we had. We could farrow a few sows in our hog house and several mares in farm stalls, but that was the limit of room we had for such births. And my father may not have wished to be involved in large-scale livestock breeding, which was labor intensive.

There were also economic reasons. Feeder cattle or sheep had to be purchased with money borrowed from a local bank. To raise them from birth required an extended loan from the bank in a period of economic distress. The change would demand new facilities and additional expenses for veterinary visits. My father, who desperately worried about money, would not have welcomed a heavier debt burden even if he could have qualified for it.

Feeder pigs were another matter. The main problem with buying them was not the cost but their propensity to get sick. We also had poor facilities for hog raising—just a twelve-pen hog house. If used for the entire cycle of raising pigs from birth to market-weight hogs, it was not sterile enough to ensure wellness. It was old, constructed of hollow tile, lacked inside feeding facilities, and was difficult to clean.

Despite these problems we regularly fattened twenty to thirty feeder pigs for a small source of income. The pigs usually came from local farms and were purchased at a nearby auction barn. They weighed anywhere from seventy-five to a hundred pounds and were usually of mixed breeds. Although vaccinated for common swine diseases, they risked exposure to other bacterial infections in their point of origin or in their short stay in the auction barn.

Since the sows usually farrowed twice a year, in the spring and in the fall, we bought feeder pigs in the late spring or early fall. Spring pigs could roam our pasture or fields in the warmer weather. They relished the first grass and tender weeds, though these stems were not major parts of their diets. Wandering on the grass gave them less exposure to harmful bacteria while the exercise furthered their health. But they could root up the soil in search of tender roots or root under fences to escape to an adjoining field, a problem solved somewhat by ringing the animal (placing a ring in the nose so that the pain of rooting would inhibit the practice). Ringing did not entirely solve the fencing problem, however, as our fences were old and could be breached by determined hogs.

Feeder pigs bought in the fall could still roam the fields but were less likely to root them up because of the frozen ground and because they tended to huddle together in their unheated quarters. They were often healthier in the wintertime because the cold weather killed bacteria and parasites. Like humans, however, the pigs were susceptible to colds and flu that came in season. They also gained weight more slowly since more calories went to keep their bodies warm.

I never was particularly fond of pigs. They were clean animals, being one of the few species that did not foul their sleeping quarters with their own manure, preferring to frequent one area in which to defecate. But they did seek out mud holes and similarly cool spots in hot weather because they had no sweat glands. They also were voracious eaters and, unlike other domestic animals with the exception of chickens, were omnivorous. They needed more protein in their diets from sources other than corn. For their protein supplement we bought tankage, consisting of processed ground-up carcasses of dead animals—highly unpleasant to smell and to feed. But hogs would eat live and dead animals too (including humans). Some might acquire a taste for chickens and attempt to catch them. And it was not uncommon for an elderly farmer to have a heart attack or faint and be set upon and eaten by his hogs.

That was unlikely for someone my age, but being attacked by hogs was not. Hogs are herd animals that come to one another's defense. A panicked squeal from one can bring the rest of the group running to help with mouths open, with terrible screams, and with the hair on their backs raised—a fearsome sight.

One of the nightmares I remember while growing up reflected an event that had once happened to me. Our feeder pigs had fallen ill with the scours, a not infrequent occurrence. The veterinarian prescribed a medicine that, when mixed with water and allowed to soak in a barrel of oats for several days, would cure the intestinal problem. But the procedure required that the hogs be confined without feed

for two days in order to sharpen their appetites for the
treated oats.

We followed his instructions, penning the animals in the
hog house until the appointed time. My father proposed a
strategy: we would herd the hogs to the back half of the hog
house, in the center aisle. Then he would fill the trough in
the front part of the aisle with the medicated feed while I,
armed with a club, held the animals at bay behind a hurdle.

Unfortunately neither of us anticipated the reaction of
these starved animals crazed by the lack of food and seemingly not hindered by their illness. They became ravenous.
They tried to climb over the barrier, squealing and fighting
with their mouths wide open while being pushed from behind by their equally famished fellows. Even throwing my
whole weight against the hurdle and beating the noses of
those climbing over to get me, I was forced back slowly and
was about to be overcome when my father, his task finished,
helped me pull the hurdle aside and allow the hogs access to
the feed. I don't remember the outcome—did the hogs re-
cover? I do remember that I did not lose control of my blad-
der or bowels, as stories circulating about other farm boys in
frightening circumstances had it, but the episode remains
vivid in my mind.

When the hogs reached optimum market weight, which
at the time was from 200 to 225 pounds, they went to local
market (we never had a large enough herd to send to larger
regional markets). We hauled the finished animals to nearby
stockyards in our trailer pulled with our car. Their sale did
not account for a major part of our farm income, but it
helped.

Not all hogs went to market; some became food for our
table. Butchering the hogs required an extended family effort, involving all my uncles. They would come with their

knives and sharpeners; my father would get out our large cast-iron cauldron, a large barrel, and a sausage grinder. He would shoot the hogs with his .22 rifle and one of my uncles, usually Freeman, would cut their throats to bleed out the blood. Then all the brothers would scald the hogs in the boiling water, a job requiring experience and judgment: too long an exposure would set the bristles, too short would not loosen them enough. If done properly, the bristles could be removed with bell-shaped scrapers, leaving the hog's hide shaved clean. If the scalding failed, a much more difficult process of skinning had to be used. This was complicated because, unlike cattle or sheep, hogs have a thick layer of fat just under their skin, which makes skinning extremely difficult.

Once scraped, the carcass was dismembered and various parts of the whole animal processed. Uncle Frank presided over the lard kettle, melting the fat and tasting the cracklings before pouring the lard into five-gallon containers to store for use. My other uncles cut up hams and shoulders to be cured by my father. My father ground scraps of meat and fat to make sausage in a small hand-powered grinder. He would pause only to add sage, pepper, and other seasonings before frying a patty to taste. He would repeat the process until it tasted right to him. My mother had little or no role in this annual ritual, which was repeated at each of my uncles' farms.

Besides pork, red meat was always a major part of our diet. We regularly had a young steer or heifer whose destiny was our table. Quite often we butchered the animal ourselves; I learned to help hoist the carcass with a block and tackle, to skin without damaging the hide, and to gut without losing the liver and heart. To butcher a good-size beef required two sets of hands. Until I could help, my father often took the steer to a professional butcher to be killed and processed. On one occasion we butchered an animal at home during the late fall and hung the carcass in a small outbuilding that usually held oats or corn but was vacant that season. The weather remained cold all winter, periods of freezing alternating with periods of thawing, never becoming very warm. That year one of my tasks was to get meat for dinner, and I would take a butcher knife and cut a steak or a roast off the carcass. The meat was wonderful!

Our feeder sheep originated in the West, though sometimes they came from the Southwest, from Texas in particular. The reason for feeding Western lambs was twofold: no local producers had enough animals to make up the usual two railroad carloads (250 sheep each) that made up the flock we wanted, and the lambs from the West came off open range and were less likely to harbor parasites. Range sheep from Texas were less desirable since they were more often infested with parasites, and they had more fine-wool blood in them. Fine-wool sheep had wrinklier necks (the wrinkles denoted more wool) and were less attractive animals. My father had an aesthetic view of all animals. He preferred good-looking specimens even if they were no more profitable than others he could have purchased.

In earlier years when my father fed cattle, my grandfather used to travel to regional stockyards to buy feeder cattle. He would get aboard an interurban that ran between Oskaloosa and Wright to catch the train to Kansas City or St. Paul. The animals he bought would be shipped by train to Wright and then collected there. In later years, after my father had switched from cattle to sheep, a commission merchant in Oskaloosa would either travel or send his son west to buy sheep. The firm, Carmichael and Son, would buy in quantity at various stops along the way, for the four Hoover brothers alone would require two thousand head (two carloads each), and they were not the sole customers.

Once back in Iowa, Carmichael would call on each brother to describe what he had bought and inquire if there were an interest in buying. He would indicate a price—for which no negotiation was allowed—and the animal's weight and place of origin: Belle Fourche, South Dakota; Mountain Home, Idaho; Bellingham, Washington—names that resonated in my mind and seemed quite exotic for someone who had never even been to Nebraska.

If my father were interested, he would go to a bank in Oskaloosa for a loan to buy the lambs. As the depression eased and he accumulated a good record of repayment, he no longer needed prior approval but could make a deal and then apply for a loan.

Once purchased, the lambs arrived by train or truck. Mostly they came by train to a little stockyard in Wright, the crossroads community two and a half miles from our farm. There were never any railway workers in the yards; when the freight train delivered the boxcars, the train men switched them to the siding, leaving us to lever the cars into an unloading position next to the fixed chutes. We either unloaded the lambs into trucks or drove them home on foot.

Famished after their long trip from the West, the lambs ate almost any green plant en route if we drove them along the gravel road. If they had no opportunity to graze on a walk to the farm, they wasted no time doing so once they arrived by truck. We had a small lot near the house that served as an unloading pen at this time. We had to be careful not to permit the lambs near any small trees or flowers as these proved most attractive to the hungry animals.

The lambs had had no experience of fences in the West and had to be educated about them. The first few days were critical: if one lamb hopped a fence, others were sure to follow.

I remember one group of lambs that were quite wild. They arrived at our farm by truck about five in the afternoon, as the sun was beginning to sink. Soon after being unloaded, they began jumping the lot fence and got onto the dirt road leading to a concrete highway that ran by our house. They split into several groups as they headed north on US 63, which had a fairly heavy traffic pattern for a road that connected several small Iowa towns.

Sheep are notoriously difficult to herd. They hang together and follow the leader but also divide into small groups. The best way to take advantage of their tendencies is to have a dog that keeps them cohesive, or a goat that may be enticed to lead them in one direction. We had neither. (My grandfather had both when he became older and couldn't move around as well as he once had. Stockyards also used so-called Judas goats.)

As we rounded them up and pushed the five hundred animals back to the farm, traffic continued along the highway, scattering the lambs as it passed. In the process of returning the lambs, I heard a loud and sickening thud: a car had hit an animal. The driver did not stop, however, and I rushed back to check on the condition of the lamb lying on the roadside. It was obviously badly injured, but since my priority was to help get the flock home, I only moved it farther off the road into the grass and weeds of the shoulder and marked the location in my mind.

When we finally settled the lambs, the sky had darkened into twilight. I took a flashlight to look for the injured animal. I searched the area thoroughly but never found it. I did not think the lamb could walk. I believe a passerby picked up the animal and took it along. The whole affair seemed an odd one to me—why would anyone steal a badly injured animal? I had never heard of roadkill at that time, but it was the depression: people often went to great lengths for food.

The loss of one lamb was not unusual; father factored deaths into his estimate of possible profits. But the manner of loss was quite unusual. We expected that the deaths of feeder lambs would be the result of overeating disease caused by an excessive amount of corn consumed.

Corn's high carbohydrate content was ill suited to ruminants such as cattle and sheep with their several stomachs genetically designed to digest the large amounts of fiber in grass and hay. Stomachs filled with corn would often prove fatal to these animals. (One of the reasons why father fed lambs instead of cattle was that the loss of one steer out of twenty often meant an end to any profit while two or three dead sheep out of five hundred was not as devastating.)

Sheep had no self-regulating mechanism to prevent them from eating too much. Few domestic animals did. Horses would founder (overeat) if given the chance; cows will overeat too. Mules and pigs, despite their reputation, would not. They would eat enough to get fat but not to get sick.

We allowed the lambs in the cornfield to eat the corn and scatter their manure—saving us two steps in their care. When the lambs first entered the field, they had no idea the corn kernel was edible. For several weeks they ate the weeds and grass in the fencerows and the lower leaves of the corn plant. The ears located at a higher level went untouched. Up to this point, the stripping of the lower leaves opened the field to air and faster drying of the corn. At some moment, however, an adventuresome sheep would discover that an ear of corn was delicious, and by some communications process all the others would learn this as well. It was at this period of discovery that the most overeating deaths occurred, though they might also happen at any time in the feeding process.

How to prevent or limit these deaths was always a major concern. One common way was to vaccinate the sheep against the disease before turning them into the fields. This seemed to mitigate deaths but was not totally effective.

Often the vaccination involved all four Hoover brothers and about two thousand sheep. On the designated day the lambs would be confined. The four brothers and their sons who were old enough to participate met with the veterinarian early in the morning. He had a bag resembling a hot water bottle hanging around his neck. Connected to the bottle was a tube running to a large syringe with a thumbscrew that when turned produced measured doses. We would catch a lamb, he would swab it behind the front leg with what appeared to be iodine and then inject a shot. As he finished, we would set another sheep on its rear end while he quickly measured out the next amount of serum. The work would be complete by the end of the day when all two thousand had received their shots.

This was not the only remedy. We tried other methods to reduce overeating deaths, such as providing alternate feed in order to diminish the craving for corn. An obvious substitute was hay when our green pasture had dried up or had stopped growing with the first frosts. We did this by throwing hay on the ground after loading it from the barn onto the hayrack. I usually drove the horses for this chore while Father pitched the loose hay off the wagon or opened hay bales to throw out slices. This was always a cold and uncomfortable job. My fingers became chilled and cramped as I tried to control the horses that were themselves cold and anxious to go. When a tractor replaced the horses, the task became easier. Using our car with a trailer was even better since the car's heater kept me warm. (It also enabled me to learn to drive a car when I was twelve.)

Still another supposed solution was to feed molasses to the lambs. I was never certain about the theory behind the practice. Perhaps the sweetness of the molasses would satisfy the lambs' hunger for corn, or perhaps molasses contained ingredients lacking in the corn that would make for a more balanced diet. In any case, we would buy molasses by the barrel and allow the lambs free access to it. Whether it was effective was again difficult to determine, but the lambs loved it.

Despite all efforts, we lost some lambs. Their deaths presented a problem that all farmers faced—how to dispose of dead animals. With small animals such as chickens, burial was easy and could be done in our small woodlot—that was my task. With larger animals such as horses or cattle, burial was a horrendous task because of the size of the hole that had to be hand dug. Even with hogs or sheep it was difficult. For these animals the answer was to call the rendering truck that hauled the carcasses away to be turned into tankage and other products.

The service was free; the carcass simply had to be moved to a designated place. Once the truck arrived, the trucker would draw up the dead animal by means of a winch. I thought the job was a horrible one, certainly smelly. But the experience taught me something about the ability of humans to adapt to even the most disagreeable circumstances: the drivers never seemed to notice the smell. One who came at lunchtime refused to leave his truck when invited to sit under a nearby tree far enough away to avoid the smell as he ate his meal. He said he no longer minded the stench.

None of the disposal solutions much helped our situation with the lambs. Most of them died in the cornfields some distance from the road and not reachable by the truck. Removing them to the pickup point would have been arduous, even if we knew where they had died. We did not regularly search the fields for dead animals.

The solution was to add hogs to the mix. The hogs would eat the dead sheep as well as the corn that the sheep had knocked on the ground or passed in semi-digested form. This way the hogs would get the needed protein to balance the carbohydrates in the corn. Their manure would also join that of the sheep to fertilize the fields, and their foraging for flesh would solve the disposal problem.

This method made it difficult to determine the death rate of the lambs, and failing to dispose of the dead animals might attract other predators. Still, it seemed the best solution available.

As the lambs fed themselves and grew fat, little remained for us to do in caring for them except to give them hay and water. We provided salt in the form of blocks, either plain or combined with wormicides, which they could lick at any time for needed minerals.

Watering five hundred head of sheep in the warm days of early fall was no small task. Before electrification a two-cycle gasoline engine provided the necessary power to fill the concrete tank that was the main source of water for all our animals. We had two other wells located nearer to outlying fields that supplied water in those areas, but these wells lacked powered pumps and any water drawn from them had to be pumped by hand. That was often my job. It is surprising how much water five hundred thirsty animals could drink. On very warm days I might hand-pump for two hours before the flock stopped drinking. On the positive side, pumping water was no more boring than working out in a gym, and at least the exercise was outdoors in clean air. It also developed biceps and shoulder muscles.

The market for lamb was in the East; few residents in Iowa or the Midwest, save those in larger cities, relished the meat. People in our area actually disliked lamb. A not atypical example of the bias came when my grandfather hired a tiler with his sons to install drainage tile in a wet spot in one field. In the course of conversation during the labor, the workers expressed their distaste for lamb as food when they saw Grandfather's flock in an adjoining field. My grandfather knew that the only meat available for the necessary noon meal was lamb and that he had no time to find a substitute. He told my grandmother not to identify the lamb but to call it "meat" when she passed the slices on a platter. After the workers praised the meal, my grandfather, who enjoyed arguments, identified the meat and referred to the crew's earlier comments. According to him, they denied them and claimed to love lamb, a face-saving lie.

We liked and ate lamb. We butchered our own, and the process became familiar enough to me that my father sometimes told me to dress a lamb by myself. The main principle involved was to be quite careful when skinning the animal to prevent the wool from touching the meat. This would keep the gamy flavor associated with mutton, the meat of older sheep, from flavoring the lamb.

But we ate less lamb than pork or beef. The lambs, after all, were our cash crop; my mother never canned lamb as she did pork and beef; and lamb was less popular with visitors. We never ate mutton because of its stronger taste, but that did not deter my grandfather or my uncle Freeman, who liked to eat it cold.

The optimum time span for selling the lambs was narrow: the weather needed to be cold and the holiday season near; the lambs had to be fat but not too fat. Moreover they could not be kept too long; if they had shed their lamb teeth and had their yearling teeth, they no longer were considered to be lambs but were priced as older sheep. (This did not prevent packers from passing off yearling meat as lamb.) The ideal weight for lambs at that time was between ninety and a hundred pounds.

A market for mutton could be found, but it was more limited. For Anglophiles a saddle of mutton was still the prime selection for holiday feasts. One could also find a few restaurants like Keen's Chophouse in New York City that offered mutton chops on the menu. (It is interesting to note that Keen's now uses large lamb chops to stand in for mutton chops, a complete switch from earlier days.)

But we sold lambs, not more mature sheep, so the decision on when to sell depended on the state of the market and the condition of the lambs. For the first, my father relied on two sources—the market reports that seemed always to be coming from our radio, and the *Chicago Drovers' Journal.* The radio reports were filler between educational programs on the radio station of Iowa State College; the *Journal* appeared every day in a full-size newspaper format and included a comic strip, ads, and feature articles often consisting of interviews with farmers who had come to the Chicago stockyards with their animals. The market reports covered the major yards in such urban centers as Chicago, Omaha, and Kansas City as well as smaller regional ones such as Albert Lea, Minnesota.

The key was to hit a rising market. Where to sell depended on the price differential between the local market, the one in Cedar Rapids, for example, and Chicago, less the expense of transportation—the cost of trucks for local markets and sometimes for Chicago as compared to the cost of rail shipment; plus commission and pen charges for hay and other necessities in Chicago that were not part of local expenses. It might also include the return passenger ticket cost from Chicago, though that was a minor item.

For judging market readiness, experience taught that the easiest way was to feel the layer of muscle and fat over the lamb's loin. Often my uncles and my father joined in making a collective judgment. Only later was my opinion consulted. Usually we sold the entire flock at one time, but sometimes we sorted the lambs into those considered market ready, or "finished," and those that required a few more weeks of feeding. This happened most often with local packing plants that required fewer lambs because of lower capacity and demand.

Once the lambs had been judged ready, the local buyer would come when contacted. A period of negotiation followed. The buyer, a man of obvious rural roots, would insist that the packinghouse had placed severe limits upon his offer. He would then agree with my father that, though the packing plant always complained about its costs, it seemed to make enough profit each year to pay dividends. Sometimes he was able to offer enough to buy the lambs he wanted. If the buyer bought the flock, my father made arrangements for local truckers to pick up the lambs. Before they arrived in their semis, we and my uncles herded the sheep into our barnlot and funneled a small number at a time into a loading chute. We prodded and pushed the animals into double-decked trucks. Then father climbed into the truck and went off to market in Cedar Rapids or Des Moines. When I became old enough, I could go as well. The trip seemed exciting to a young boy, but in retrospect it was quite ordinary, taking only a few hours to arrive and culminating in lunch in a cheap restaurant near the yards.

Going to Chicago was another matter entirely. In the early 1930s the lambs went by freight train, but later the choice was to truck them all the way. The main reason for the change seemed to be the poor rail connection to Chicago that involved several switchings and a long delay in arrival.

Even though rail shipping cost less, the delay and subsequent weight loss, not to mention the inconvenience, more than balanced the price advantage.

The truck ride to Chicago proved very exciting to me when my father permitted me to go as a teenager. I had rarely been out of Iowa and had never before visited a large city. Even though my view of the city was pretty constricted, I found it thrilling and awe-inspiring, not to say frightening. I think my view of the city was not atypical: danger lurked around every corner, waiting to snare the unwary, innocent farm boy.

Neither the farms we saw en route nor the yards in Chicago, despite their size, appeared unfamiliar, but the city itself did. When my two uncles, Freeman and Carl, and I arrived, they contacted a commission firm that was to handle the sale. The firm arranged to have the animals placed in its pens and to have them fed and watered (Uncle Carl always complained of the cost of the hay, which was at least four times more expensive than back home in Iowa). After the animals had been settled, we went to stay at the Stockyards Inn, not in the upscale hotel with its fine restaurant but in a large room with a series of bunk beds and a hall tree for clothes. We all claimed bunks; I took an upper bunk but my uncles got lower ones. I fell asleep almost at once, but when I awoke the next day I found Uncle Freeman gone from his bed. Uncle Carl and I, quite concerned, looked for him and finally found him sitting and looking disgusted in a chair in the lobby. He told us a drunken guest had stepped on his face when trying to climb into the upper bunk, and he hadn't been able to get back to sleep.

In the holding pens we waited for the buyers for the major packing plants to arrive. Atop horses, they rode by the pens wearing boots and carrying whips, looking very grand

and in control. A more prosaic reason for the horses and boots was the messy, manure-covered aisles that traversed the yards. The buyers addressed the commission firm representative in the pens to negotiate. The representative bargained primarily about price but he also argued about such matters as when the animals would be taken off feed and water. Once a deal was struck, he would also negotiate a time that the sheep could be weighed with the weigh master. All these concerns centered on the lambs' weight; the packing plant did not wish to pay the weight of hay and water, and the owner did not want his animals to shrink while waiting to be weighed.

If there was no great backlog of animals waiting to be weighed, and if our lot had been sold early enough in the day, we could collect the check with the commission deducted immediately. Otherwise the commission firm would mail the check to our Iowa address. In either case our responsibilities were ended, and we had time to taste the wonders of Chicago fleshpots before returning home. These consisted of visits to a soda fountain to sample a chocolate malted milk, and to a newsreel theater. The malted we could get at home; the newsreel we could not. Then we headed home.

For me, whatever the calendar might say, autumn ended when our feeder lambs were gone. This might be at Thanksgiving or later, before Christmas. It always ended before the New Year. Winter was coming, a time to get ready for spring planting.

Field day at our farm, a special occasion. I am third from the left with my sister Alice to my left. My cousins Louise and Herbert are to my right. The hand at the right of the photo belongs to the county agent who is judging the lambs by feeling the loin.

Respite: An Agricultural Education

🌾 AUTUMN ALSO MEANT a return to school. Every year after I was five, I looked forward to the opening of classes. I graduated eighth grade from a rural school and then attended a high school in nearby Oskaloosa.

My agricultural education had three sources: the first was my father, uncles, and grandfather, and my immersion in everyday life and work; the second was from farm neighbors, particularly boys my age as I observed their family practices or talked with them as we walked to the country school, where there were few if any formal lessons on agriculture; and the third was hands-on organizations like 4-H and Future Farmers of America (FFA), the latter closely affiliated with the vocational education classes I took in high school.

My first formal education was at the Bloomfield School in Spring Creek Township. The Northwest Ordinance of 1787 had set the standard for education in the Midwest by setting aside one section in a township for education. When I was growing up in Iowa, each township in Mahaska County had a one-room school. While township officials ran the schools insofar as maintaining buildings, setting budgets, and hiring teachers, the county ultimately supervised and controlled these institutions. A county superintendent set curriculums, maintained standards, and advised county officials on like matters. Finally the county could decide, as it did in Iowa and other states in the 1940s and 1950s, to eliminate these schools and consolidate the students in new, larger units.

The school that my sisters and I attended was not the one in the township where we lived. Our farm lay at the extreme northeast corner of Harrison Township, so we should have gone to the Red School several miles away. But there was no easy way for us to get there, either on foot or by other means. The new concrete highway, US 63, angled south and east, adding several miles to any trip to the Red School. It was possible for us to walk across one of our fields, climb over a fence into a neighbor's field, cross a creek, go through his farmyard, and intersect a dirt road. But this much shorter route had a number of serious disadvantages. One was mud—in the spring, after the thaw, the mud was both deep and sticky. The creek was another—it was shallow and lacked a bridge, and in winter the ice could not be trusted to support someone walking on it. A third problem was the neighbor's barnyard. Like most other farmers, he owned dogs, and these always seemed to be small ones—the most treacherous, I think, likely to sneak up behind you and nip your heels. Twice as I was crossing his yard, one of these bit me. The nip startled me so that I tripped over a rock and fell down in the driveway. The neighbor, Henry de Boef, flew out of his house to tackle the dog, saving me from more severe wounds (but with torn clothes).

Because our possible routes to the Red School seemed impracticable, my parents chose to send us instead to the Bloomfield School in Spring Creek Township, which abutted Harrison to the north. The transfer cannot have been difficult to arrange as my two uncles, Carl and Dick, served on the school board.

The route to the Bloomfield School was superior—shorter by a good deal, and safer. It took us on two roads, the first crushed rock and the other dirt, directly to the school but at a right angle. Neither had traffic like US 63, and while the second leg of the route could be muddy, it was less so than the route through the fields. But the walk to the Bloomfield School provided company as well. On two adjoining farms, children our age went to that school, and several others would join our walk farther along the way. In good weather we could walk together; in bad our parents could take us in a shared car.

For me at least, going to this school furthered a sense of family or tribal unity. My uncles had at least partial control over the school, and my cousins, second cousins, and my sister and I constituted at least half the students in attendance. In addition, across the road from the schoolyard was Bloomfield Friends Church, where my family were members and attended until it closed and our devotions moved to my grandparents' house. The graveyard behind the church contains many relatives, Hoovers and others, who in death outnumbered those still living. I felt a sense of our encompassing community located on that Iowa hill.

Bloomfield School was an island in the country with no other structure save the Friends Church in the area. Everything else was farmland, pasture and crop-filled.

The schoolyard probably encompassed an acre of grass lawn bordered by trees. The only playground equipment in the yard were a swing set and a seesaw. In front of the schoolhouse was a well with a pump, and in back two outhouses, one for each sex. A county road ran on the south side and another on the west side of the schoolyard while a fence on the north and east sides kept the cows in the pasture from the school property.

All of us in school were familiar with rural life, students and teachers alike. We were quite unsophisticated in many ways, but we shared a common background. Providing programs for parents at times like Christmas was part of the job for the teachers who, like Miss Anderson, the one I most remember, were young, unmarried, and had gone to a summer training program after high school graduation. Their duties included cleaning the building, starting the fire in the morning, and supervising the general condition of the school property. Of course they called upon students to help.

One of the tasks Miss Anderson gave me (I was one of her pets because I was shy and hence always well behaved) when I became older was to inspect the boy's outhouse after school for graffiti. At the time a neighboring farmer's son, Joe Gray, would walk over the fields to visit her after school, and she feared there were obscene drawings, portraying these trysts, left by boys in the facility. I never found any, nor did I quite understand her reluctance to enter the outhouse after everyone else had left.

Such were the patterns of rural courtship, also a learning experience for me. Joe and Miss Anderson eventually married; she went to live on the farm and opened an antique shop in their henhouse.

Soon after beginning primary grade (essentially kindergarten), I moved into first grade because of my reading ability. The work was easy and the system, given the fact there were only about twenty students of varying ability in the entire school, arranged in nine classes (primary through eighth grade), fairly efficient. Assigned a separate desk, we all had our own books that our parents had purchased for us along with basic supplies. Here we studied until the teacher called for our class to come to the recitation bench. There she quizzed us over the assigned material before sending us back to our individual desks and calling up the next group.

None of the material in our textbooks applied to our farm life. There was no specific reference to any farming experience or to agricultural science. I imagine that our curriculum varied little from that in urban areas except for the almost virtual absence of instruction in music and art. We also lacked organized physical education, but we got plenty of exercise.

There had been little change in the structure or practice of education from the time my father and uncles had attended the Bloomfield School. Old sepia photographs taken in their day showed them lined up against the west wall of the school and seemed almost identical with those taken of me with my classmates twenty or more years later. The left-over curricular material appeared familiar too.

But there had been some changes. The school was a much more civil and peaceful place in my day than in my father's. In his time, boys who were as old as eighteen attended the winter session (the school had had three sessions a year—fall, winter, and spring) and bullied the younger boys. These grown men once threw my father out the front door and broke his leg. In my day the school had no such sessions but met for one nine-month period, and no older boys remained as pupils after the age of fourteen, even if they had not graduated from the eighth grade.

Despite its evolution, the school retained its rural character. We could watch the cows in the adjoining pasture and try to drown the ground squirrels in another. One of our classmates, Glen Pringle, ran a trapline in the winter before coming to school, and not infrequently tangled with civet cats or skunks. The smell he picked up permeated our over- heated room, to our considerable discomfort.

Another student, Donald Fallis, rode a pony to school for a few years. My sister and I rode a horse for part of a year until the horse jumped grader ditches in a race with the pony. We tethered the animals on an old hitching rail in the churchyard while classes met. In free time we could tend the horses and seemingly imagine we were back at home.

The Bloomfield School served as the center of the rural community, at least as far as those families with children were concerned, just as the Friends Church had done before city churches siphoned off its membership. School programs and other events such as school picnics brought families together with a sense of unified experience and common purpose.

In these meetings and in our walks to school I could see reminders of the past in the farms and farmers I encoun- tered. I could see both the changes that had already oc- curred and those that were still taking place. I also became friends with boys of my own generation who, like me, would leave farming for other pursuits.

The Fallis farm lay across from ours, divided by US 63. Dick Fallis farmed it first as I was growing up. He had one son, Donald, and a daughter named Dorothy. Donald was slightly younger than I, and we were friends through high school; Dorothy died while still in grade school.

The Fallises had lived in the area for several generations and displayed great family solidarity. Dick farmed in a con- ventional way with an emphasis on grain production, mostly corn, and with a few animals to work and to sell. After a while he moved to a rented farm to allow his brother Lee Fal- lis to operate the old place. After World War II he took a job at a packing plant in Ottumwa, a town thirty miles south, driving pigs from truck to pen. While working days at the packing plant, he farmed at night and on weekends. When my father had to stop farming for reasons of health, Dick bought our farm and pretty much eliminated animal operations in favor of grain production so that he could continue to work in the packing plant.

Lee farmed much as his brother had on the Fallis home farm, but he raised more hogs and grew soybeans as well. He also added a small house to the homestead for his unmarried sister, following an older custom of building a residence for parents or other kin nearby to enable them to remain in a familiar setting with economic and emotional support. Lee remained at the home place, farming the same way until he retired.

Another farm next to ours belonged to the Rooy family—the father George, the mother Jeanette, two sons, Martin John and Sidney, and two daughters, Joan and Shirley. They were Dutch. George had worked in a New Jersey shipyard during World War I before buying a small farm next to ours. He had moved to Iowa as part of a Dutch community that was expanding south from Pella, a community of Christian Reform church members, more theologically conservative than the Dutch Reform church.

The Rooys were conventional farmers who combined crop raising with a few animals such as pigs and cows. My father regarded their family operation as lacking the skills of one with more historical experience behind it. Although the Rooys had newer equipment than ours because of their later entry into farming, and bought a tractor as early as most others in the area, they seemed to be less adroit in using the machines and more accident prone.

Martin and Sidney were boys closest in age to me, and also in closest proximity for purposes of play. Martin was more than a year older while Sidney was a day younger than I, a matter of pride for me and chagrin for him. We occasionally played ball together in the Rooy pasture, using cow chips for bases, usually at twilight after chores. But this was an uncommon occurrence, for the Rooy boys had to work hard—as we all did.

The Rooy house was the first stop on the two-mile walk to school. We walked together for a mile on a crushed-rock road without houses before turning onto the dirt road where we would see family farms again. On the second mile there were seven such farms.

This mile-long row of houses contained those of families that were longtime residents as well as those of a few newcomers. The road had fewer cars and pedestrians, and was narrower with shallower ditches. Fences and buildings were closer to it. The route also seemed to contain relics of an earlier time.

The first house on the right along the dirt road to school belonged to an older, semi-retired farmer whose small lot next to his house displayed a row of obsolete machinery that included an old steam engine. It never moved but remained in the open air winter and summer, rusting away.

The next house, on the left, belonged to the Pringle family, whose members were relatives of mine. Alvin Pringle, the patriarch, had married my grandmother's sister Tressie and farmed the land until he turned the operation over to his son Ralph.

Alvin was the same age as my grandfather but was to outlive him. Almost blind, he lived with Tressie in a small house built next door to the farmhouse in the same fashion that Lee Fallis's sister did on the Fallis farm. When Tressie died, Alvin moved to live with a daughter in town until he died in his nineties.

Ralph farmed much the same way his father did; he seemed to me to epitomize an earlier, old-fashioned age. Even his work clothes (I never saw him in anything else) exemplified that. He dressed in overalls and a work shirt like everyone else, but, unlike them, he wore a red bandanna around his neck and a straw hat, a fashion of thirty years earlier.

His farming methods too were of an earlier age. Ralph was the only farmer I knew who still pastured his cows alongside the road, where his younger son watched after them. Although the road had little except local traffic, the cows faced the danger of being struck by a car or truck since they wandered slowly across the road as they searched for more palatable grass. And Ralph did not mechanize; I never knew him to own a tractor.

Ralph and his wife Fannie died in a house fire before I left our farm. The circumstances of their deaths were curious, and rumors spread of household friction leading to tragedy.

Beyond the Pringle farm was the Crosier farmstead. The Crosier family had been residents for several generations and were an established farming family. Their farmstead consisted of the standard farm buildings—barn, corncrib, hog house, and so forth—on one side of the road and a small tenant or hired man's house on the other along with a small garden patch. While I went to grade school the small house was occupied. I remember the music that poured out of the tenant house. It was what we then called hillbilly music (now renamed country and western), and those who listened to it often were relegated by neighbors to a lower social class such as hired laborers.

Harry Crosier was a bachelor who required extra labor because he had no family to help work his farm. He was the

only farmer I knew at the time who had separate living
arrangements for hired help. The small house allowed the
hired man to have a family and be more than just temporary
help.

I knew that the Crosier farm would soon be history.
There was no one to carry on what had been a family tradition. Elsie Crosier, Harry's sister, had become a nurse but
had never married. The farm was sold into other hands when
Harry died, at a time when I still lived at home.

The last farm on the road to school belonged to the Taylor family but changed hands even before the Crosier farm.
Estell Taylor had a general-purpose farm like Crosier's but
became interested in raising hybrid seed corn when that in-
novation in crop raising became commercially feasible. He
sold that farm and bought a larger one several miles away to
concentrate on establishing a seed corn business, using as
base stock seeds he obtained from Iowa State College.

I learned from the walks to school of older ways of farming and of the new ways replacing them. Older farmers—
the steam engine owner, Harry Crosier, and the Pringles—
represented an approach to agriculture that was fading
away. They would not be replaced by their kind. Dick Fallis
and Estell Taylor presaged a future agriculture. Fallis had
become the part-time farmer who worked a small piece of
land for fewer hours a week while depending on an outside,
nonagricultural job for his livelihood. Taylor, on the other
hand, anticipated the day of greater specialization, earning
his living by concentrating on one crop that required special
knowledge and different techniques.

BEGINNING in 1936 I became a member of an organization
dedicated to agricultural education, the 4-H club, where I
learned this little affirmation:

I pledge
My head to clearer thinking
My heart to greater loyalty
My hands to larger service
My health to better living
For my club, my community, my country
And my world.

I must have repeated this 4-H pledge over a hundred times in my decade of membership. It was a pledge that interpreted what the four Hs in the clover emblem of the club represented, and it was reiterated at every club meeting. Since one could enter the club at age ten and "graduate" at twenty-one, membership could and did extend over one's entire adolescence and early adulthood. It did in my case.

Three organizations relating to the education of farmers—the county extension service, the Farm Bureau, and 4-H—seemed to intertwine so that even now I have difficulty distinguishing among them. The county extension agent participated in important 4-H events and encouraged membership in that youth group as well as in the Farm Bureau; the Farm Bureau in turn utilized the expertise of the county extension agent and provided education and services to families of members; and 4-H club members came largely from those families belonging to the Farm Bureau. All three appeared to me to be branches of the same tree.

Then in 1939, when I started attending Oskaloosa High School, I became a member of another educational organization for aspiring farmers, Future Farmers of America. This group paralleled the 4-H clubs. One chief difference was that FFA members were mainly high school students while 4-H members encompassed a broader age group.

The Smith-Hughes Act of 1917 had sought to promote agricultural education in American high schools. It had been neglected in traditional high schools, and the attempt to increase student retention and enrollment added more vocational courses to the curriculum. The goal was to prepare those "who have entered upon or who are preparing to enter upon the work of the farm." The act encouraged schools to offer agricultural courses and to have trained teachers for those courses. Federal funds helped support the program in a variety of ways, including teacher salary supplements.

Oskaloosa High School took part in the federal program, offering vocational agriculture courses for its students. It provided classrooms and one teacher for a series of classes on agriculture and allowed the organization of an FFA chapter as an interest group. The instructor of the ag classes served as the group's sponsor, and most of the students in the classes were also members of the FFA.

The FFA experience began and ended primarily in high school, a four-year period, unless the members were so outstanding as to hold state or national office. As was the case with 4-H and the county extension service, FFA and agricultural classes became conflated in my mind, two aspects of the same thing.

Both 4-H and FFA pushed members' projects, but FFA lacked the exhibition of projects that was the culmination of 4-H work. Extension agents and vocational education teachers visited farms in the summer, but the extension agent came more often and was more visible.

Membership differed too. Girls could be 4-H club members and even have animal projects in boys' clubs, though some 4-H clubs were exclusively for girls and emphasized domestic skills. No girls were enrolled in vocational agricultural classes or in FFA. On the other hand, the boys in those classes or in FFA were not always from farms. Some had enrolled for other reasons. They might be less interested in the school's formal classes, or might harbor the hope of one day living on a farm. Some regarded the classes as part of their vocational education, to be taken in conjunction with manual training courses in wood- or metalworking. Part of the reason for their inclusion also lay in the nature of FFA. It served as an organization for farm boys who were often left out of the social hierarchy in high school. (There was always a prejudice toward the rural students among the more prominent city student leaders and sometimes even among the teachers. I recall being late for an academic class one day and being asked by the teacher what happened. "Did the cow kick over the milk pail?") FFA activities offered participation to those who were not asked to join the mainstream school groups because of social class or other differences. A member could play organized basketball or compete in speaking contests for the FFA, as I did. So varied were the opportunities that FFA sometimes earned the title "Fathers Farm Alone" because their sons were at some FFA event.

My major contact with the extension service was with the agricultural agent who visited our farm periodically to look at my and my sisters' 4-H projects. He would also be much in evidence during the field days when we visited other farms to see other 4-H projects and during the county fair when we showed our projects. My sisters had less contact with the home extension agent since they rarely exhibited anything such as food preparation or sewing work at the fair.

My experience with the Farm Bureau consisted primarily of attending the monthly and special meetings of the group with my parents. These meetings had an informational component coming from the extension service or WOI, the radio station and voice of Iowa State College. There were social components as well, sometimes homemade entertainment and always refreshments. The hostess of the evening would outdo herself in providing cakes, pies, or cookies to demonstrate her baking skills.

My 4-H experiences remain with me far more than those from FFA, perhaps because they began earlier and lasted longer.

Aimed at training youngsters in learning the theories and methods of successful farming, 4-H evolved at about the same time as the agricultural extension service and the American Farm Bureau, with much the same goals but a different clientele. No early clubs had members who lived other than on farms. Today's urban 4-H clubs would have been unimaginable in my time.

My club, the Harrison Hustlers, met once a month in members' homes with an adult sponsor. It was a township club whose membership could include anyone who lived in that area and met all the membership requirements. My club was not composed of classmates from grammar school since the Bloomfield School lay in a different township. With the exception of my cousin Herbert, I knew few of the other members of the Harrison Hustlers before joining the club.

The social aspects of the meetings remain the most vivid to me. Given the nature of boys, these were usually raucous and boisterous. (I shudder now to think how much of a trial we must have been to our volunteer sponsors.) Our formal meeting had an educational component, varying in content and detail. A look at the record of the July 1940 meeting of the Harrison Hustlers shows that all but one member attended and that the meeting's business consisted entirely of an examination of members' record books (diaries of our projects) by Mr. Stamp, the county agent. This checking anticipated the deadline of August 4 when all record books of county members were to be submitted for judging.

The girls' clubs had an equally educational program content, as shown by a sample from the same summer. On June

21 my sister Alice met with other members of the Harrison Zippers and had to answer roll call by telling how to add color to her room. She then participated by presenting ways to keep family shoes off the floor. The other participant, my cousin Phyllis, discussed footstools, and all the girls marbleized paper.

Then came refreshments and a period of play. For boys the "play" often consisted of roughhousing since the meetings were held at night and since, at the start, all homes lacked electric lights, so it was too dark to have organized sports. Sometimes we were too rough. One family of boys with brittle bones suffered several broken ones from falling or being pushed down at meetings, thus illustrating one of the problems of 4-H clubs. The mingling of preteen boys with full-grown men made for possible physical and emotional disparities and was terminated in the mid-1940s.

The heart of 4-H was the project—to learn by doing, as we were often reminded. In the beginning, 4-H club projects usually involved livestock raising and corn growing for boys and food preservation for girls. The girls' clubs expanded in the 1930s to include other homemaking skills such as the selection and construction of clothes and home management. For boys, new additions included soil conservation, tractor maintenance, electricity, and farm management.

The only project I ever had was livestock. I don't recall a different project for any members of my club either, not even corn growing. I think I know why: corn raising and other crop production involved more complicated and difficult arrangements in project isolation and development.

Crop production required more commitment, skill, and effort than animal raising. First, a 4-H member would not likely be allowed to manage a separate piece of crop land in a field that was already in production. That land was too valuable to risk crop losses in a time of depression. Second, the necessary preparation, seeding, cultivation, and harvesting might well be beyond the strength of even a teenage boy in the case of horses, or judgment in the case of tractors.

The later project additions came before many farmers had acquired a tractor or electricity. I know we had neither in 1936 when I joined my first 4-H club. A year before that, only a small minority of farms, 15 percent or fewer, had been electrified in the Midwest and only a larger minority had tractors.

Nor did we possess a row-crop tractor until late in the 1930s, and my father co-owned it with three of his brothers. Because of that fact and because of fear that I might damage the tractor, I was not allowed to do much with it except drive. Tractor maintenance would not have been a likely project for me or, I suspect, for many of my fellow 4-H members.

Farm management and soil conservation might have been suitable projects, but they lacked popularity with club leaders and the county agent whose main interests were in raising animals. They were a less tangible project to show at the county or state fairs. The end product of a project of this sort was a display board with photographs and captions— a static affair.

Projects involving animal raising were the easiest to fit into existing farm practice. The animal selected for a project usually came from a flock already on the farm—a pig from a litter, a colt from a draft mare, a lamb from a flock, or a calf from a cattle herd. The animal could easily be identified and cared for, even by a ten-year-old. And it need not be sepa-rated from the other animals of the same group.

An animal could also serve as both a 4-H and an FFA project. The basic requirements of the two organizations overlapped considerably. The principal difference was that the 4-H animal had an opportunity to be shown to the public at a fair while, at the time, the FFA had no such public exhibits. I remember quite vividly one such project.

My father had decided to use our small orchard, the one with apple and pear trees, as a place to put a small hog house, a structure that could shelter a sow with her litter of pigs. The location of the trees made mowing the area difficult, and he may have thought that the sow and little pigs would do a better job of clipping the grass. The experience did not last long. The pigs smelled bad and the clank of the lid on the hog feeder intruded too much into our lives; but for a time that was the locale for my pig project. I raised the pigs for FFA and showed them at the county fair for 4-H.

At the time, my FFA teacher in high school was Theodore Roosevelt Collins, known as Ted. He did not resemble in the least the county agents who also came to inspect the progress of our projects. They looked as if they could have been farmers. The clothes they wore—short-sleeve shirts and khaki pants—were city clothes, but they could pass for those worn by more prosperous farmers to meetings in town. More important, the county agents wore high-top shoes or boots suited to an encounter with a patch of mud or an occasional bit of manure. They were not fat, and their skins were tanned. It seemed obvious that they spent most of their time out of the office and in the field.

Mr. Collins, on the other hand, conveyed a sense of being soft. He was a large and pudgy man who moved slowly and spoke deliberately. He dressed in a citified manner, wearing better-quality clothes than most farmers could afford. His shoes were especially good looking but ill suited to tramping through a hog lot. He was not tanned; he looked like a clerk in a shoe store, which in fact he was on weekends.

But Mr. Collins said he had always wanted to be a farmer. He had married a farm girl in hopes of inheriting a farm, only to learn she had no desire to live in the country. Despite his claim, he never seemed very familiar with farm practices. He inherited the high school's vocational agriculture classes when the teacher originally leading them moved up in the FFA organization.

An incident that occurred when he visited my pig project in our orchard disillusioned me. Dressed as usual in city clothes, he walked among the fruit trees with me. By some mischance we came between the sow and her piglets, one of whom squealed—a distress signal. This brought its mother charging with a chomping jaw and a challenging roar. While not as formidable as a boar, she was nonetheless quite fearsome. Mr. Collins somehow managed to get behind *me* as we backed away from her fury. The move struck me as unseemly and less than heroic, though it was probably quite a smart thing to do. I should have known better than to get into such a position, but so should he.

I regarded the classes he taught as being more theoretical and less practical than what I learned from 4-H leaders and county agents, who used hands-on methods. Not that the theoretical was useless. One lesson I learned that served me well throughout my nonfarm life came from his discussion of Thoreau. Mr. Collins recounted the story of the writer meeting a farmer along the road who figuratively carried his farm on his back, and it caused me to think of the burden that farm ownership could be. It seemed to me at the time, when World War II had not yet ended the Great Depression, that that farmer could have been my father. The story provoked me to question whether I wanted a similar load on my back.

Both 4-H and FFA projects had paper requirements. 4-H required a record of the member's experience, in this case including the animal's rations and training, and other relevant information. It also was to contain an essay that described the most significant experience and lessons learned in the project. The completed record was then submitted for judgment and prizes.

My sister and I prepared our records after the fact. We calculated the individual rations from a division of the total given to our family's flock of lambs (fifteen to twenty-two) that we raised. We estimated answers to other questions, completing our records at the last moment before the local fair competition.

Despite our neatness and careful writing, we never received a significant award for our work. We did each earn a pencil for a completed record book. I came to believe that our problem was not the improvisation of our projects but the lack of time we spent on presentation. Those who won usually had superior features in their record books—better photographs, added pages, and a more handsome overall appearance. Another life lesson!

The record-keeping requirement for 4-H projects fit well with at least part of what was taught in our vocational agriculture classes. Exercises in calculating the food value of various animal rations, as well as the optimum quantity to be fed for the most productive results at the least expense, were valuable. But our most important goal was to win at the 4-H fair. This would be the culmination of our efforts and summer. The two fairs we aimed for were the Southern Iowa Fair at Oskaloosa in early August and the Iowa State Fair at Des Moines later that month.

The addition of 4-H clubs to the already existing fair program had created problems of barn space, competition with adult breeders, and a congested fair calendar. Some officials suggested that 4-H projects not be attached to county or state fairs but rather be held as separate events such as "field days." These were already common during the summer as

4-H members visited one another's farms to view projects. But limited participation and the lack of facilities to host large groups on individual homesteads made "field days" an inadequate substitute for the larger and better-attended fairs, which had established facilities and a scheduled time on annual farm calendars. Governing boards of the fairs also recognized that the 4-H projects brought increased attendance as fond parents followed their children's projects to the fair.

The solution was in effect to hold two fairs at the same time. The 4-H fair usually came first on the schedule, with free admission for all. Judging ended in a few days, at which time the 4-H animals were either sold or taken home to be replaced in the pens by those to be shown by adult breeders in open classes. (Open classes were largely for purebred stock shown by breeders who wished to advertise their farms.)

Most 4-H members showed only so-called market livestock in their part of the fair. Most farmers did not raise purebreds, so their children, who took their animals from already existing flocks on the farm, could not compete in classes for breeding stock. More important, 4-H members earned money from the auction sale of their market animals at the end of their part of the fair. This provided a tangible reward for their work that was greater than selling in the open market. (Bidders representing businesses connected to farming supported 4-H by bidding up sale prices.) A champion steer or pig might bring double or triple the amount earned in the open market by a bid from a feed company or a similar local business eager to show its support.

Some 4-H members, however, also showed purebred animals in open classes following the 4-H exposition. Although ours was a small farm and did not specialize in the sale of breeding stock, I showed market lambs and pigs in 4-H competition but also showed Shropshire sheep and mules (which, of course, could never be purebred) in open classes as well. I also showed a purebred Jersey heifer in both 4-H and open classes.

Preparation for the fair began early. With both market lambs and pigs, the maturity of the animal was crucial. The show animals needed to be fat (then not a dirty word) but not too fat. They had to have enough fat to give them a firm and attractive appearance with no hint of that fat limiting their activity. This was particularly true of my market lambs since I would show them first at the Southern Iowa Fair and then at the Iowa State Fair. They needed to be fat enough to win at the first but then really hit their peak at the second. I did not show pigs at the Iowa State Fair, so the hogs had to be at their best at the Southern Iowa Fair.

Market lambs and pigs were shown before they were a year old; baby beeves were supposed to be less than two years old when shown. Members sometimes purchased calves to feed as well as raising them from birth, and rumors abounded that some of these animals were older than their owners claimed. But true age proved difficult to determine.

My sister Alice showed nothing but sheep, so all the other animals to be shown became my projects. This proved fortunate for me since she always beat me in the show ring with her lambs. Early on in my first year of 4-H, my father gave Alice first choice of lambs from our flock to call hers. She chose well and in 1937 won the prize for the grand champion fat lamb at the Iowa State Fair. The next year it was my turn for first choice. I think I chose well, but I will never know. My lamb seemed the best in August, but shortly before the fair he died suddenly, probably of the heat. I felt deeply frustrated that I would have no chance to win the purple ribbon for the first time. Meanwhile Alice won again at the Iowa

State Fair, an unprecedented double. The next year she did it again, a historic triple.

The show ring was the end of a long process that involved considerable effort. The chosen animal had to endure the usual treatment of other baby animals—vaccination, castration for males if designated for market classes, tail amputation for lambs, weaning, and necessary medications such as wormicides at regular intervals. Then its diet, growth, and health needed to be closely monitored. Despite all this attention, animals such as my prize pick might die before they ever reached the fair.

As the animal grew, training began for show-ring performance. When showing calves or mules, training involved teaching the animal to accept a halter and then to learn to be led at an even pace when walking or running. Training colts to the halter often was difficult. All young animals could be cranky, particularly if they were hungry, tired, or out of sight of their mothers. Sometimes even the sight of a halter could infuriate them. Once, as my father entered the stall of a young mule with a halter in his hand, the mule began to back up, all the while kicking aggressively while my father was still behind him. He hit my father in the face, skinning his chin and nose. After this experience, I haltered the mule with great care.

With lambs the training involved the exhibitor as much as the animal. At that time no one used a halter to lead sheep in the show ring; the accepted method was to grasp the skin of the animal under the lower jaw with one hand while pushing on the rear end with the other. Even with experienced exhibitors, showing a sheep in this fashion proved difficult as exemplified by the occasional loose animals running around the ring. Young hands tired and animals fidgeted, so the failure to hold them was not unexpected. (Today sheep can be shown with rope halters, which are much more secure.) Finally, both colts and lambs needed to be trained to stand still with their legs straight and placed at the corners of their bodies while the judges studied them.

Pigs were different. Their behavior in the ring always surprised me since they are the most intelligent of domestic animals and the most nearly human in their physical confirmation. They make excellent pets and housebreak themselves. Yet they are most difficult to show, perhaps because of their independence and stubbornness. They go where they want, when they want. The showperson can only hope to steer them in a desired direction by means of a cane, a small whip, or a hurdle—and the maneuvering works only part of the time. Often the result is a melee that can be quite funny. Once, my pig ran under a judge and carried the struggling man several yards across the ring. I was not about to win anyway, so my amusement did not hurt my chances. Given the behavior of pigs, there was no advantage in attempting to train them for the show arena.

Cosmetic preparation for showing fair animals did not require much time except for sheep. Calves and mules needed brushing and combing. They would also have their hair trimmed or clipped and their hooves cut if necessary. Mules would have their manes reduced to a length of one to two inches (so the coarse hair would stand up) and the base of their tails shaved for about three to four inches. The manes and tails of horses were not shorn but were combed or braided, sometimes with rosettes.

With lambs, preparation took more time, primarily because of their wool. In fine-wooled breeds such as Merinos or Columbias, the lanolin in the fleece had to be preserved or even enhanced. We did not raise these breeds because of the depressed wool market but raised coarse-wooled breeds instead for their meat. I remember those who did show these sheep using blowtorches to singe the outer layers of the wool in order to concentrate the oils. The smell of the scorched wool also remains in my olfactory memory, always associated with the sheep barn at the Iowa State Fair.

Our Shropshire and Southdown lambs required more work. Practice at the time dictated that the animals present a rectangular appearance achieved by "blocking"—trimming the wool to show a flatter and wider back, and a flatter side, in order to emphasize the size and contour of the hindquarters. (All these areas contained the choicest lamb cuts in the retail market.) Unlike the fine-wooled breeds, coarse-wooled sheep had short fibers and much less of a fleece.

To block sheep, something needed to hold the animal while the blocker worked. We made a blocking table which consisted of a wooden platform with one end fitted with a semi-circular iron band that had a leather strap attached. The lamb stood on the table with the strap adjusted around its neck. There was no standard model; each exhibitor built his own version of the equipment.

Next, the lamb needed to be prepared for trimming. Here there were several schools of thought about the extent of washing the wool. Washing eliminated most of the lanolin, and though the market lamb's value lay in its carcass, the quality of its fleece affected its appearance and added value when sold—all factors taken into account by the judges. Some exhibitors did a full body wash that left the wool a lighter-colored white without the yellow tint given the wool by lanolin. We never did; we washed the rear end stained by urine and areas that had been dirtied by other agents. Unlike the whiter lambs, ours were grey-white in color with areas of lighter and darker wool.

The blocking tools included a wool card and shears, both traditional instruments that had been used for centuries. To begin the blocking, the wool had to be moistened and then carded. The card pulled and straightened the wool fibers, allowing the blocker to trim off the uneven ends and to create a smooth, even surface. One operation was never enough; the blocker had to go back several times to get the desired effect. My father was an excellent blocker, skillful and patient even to the point of perfection. Although he allowed me to practice, he never permitted me to do a complete job. (This cost me an award when I was in a showmanship contest at the Iowa State Fair and was asked if I had blocked the lamb I was exhibiting. I faced a quandary: I could not say yes truthfully, but if I said no, I believed I would be certain to lose. I said no and lost. I don't know what others said, but I do know that very few of my peers actually blocked their animals. The show-ring appearance was too important to be left to ten- or twelve-year-old kids.) The intervention of parents in their children's projects has a long history: the mother who writes her son's English essay or the father who yells at the umpire at Little League games is not a new type.

After blocking the sheep at home, we put homemade covers on them to try to preserve their appearance. These "blankets" were made of readily available materials—burlap bags or old canvas—that covered the body and fastened around the legs to keep them in place. Commercial "blankets" could be purchased that included hoods to fit over the lambs' heads with eyeholes and sometimes the breeder's name on them. We never had these deluxe versions, and those who did were mostly the larger, more prosperous breeders.

Despite the "blankets," our preparation at home never proved sufficient. At the fair the process had to be repeated before going to the show ring. Visitors to the fair, especially the younger ones, persisted in sticking their fingers into the wool and thus destroying the carefully crafted exterior look; or an animal would succeed in shedding its cover or mussing up its wool in some way and require a redo. Blocking seemed to be interminable and led to my sense of great boredom even while in the fair's stimulating atmosphere.

Preparing other animals at the fair proved to be easier and less time-consuming. With pigs, the usual routine was to wash the animals, then spray the hair and hooves with water, oil, or fly spray to make those parts shine. My cousin Herbert, who showed Chester White hogs, added another feature. In order to accentuate the hogs' whiteness, he bought cheap talcum powder from the five-and-ten-cent store to sprinkle on them. It did make the pigs seem whiter, but the smell of the cheap talc mixed with hog manure gave me sensory overload.

Slick-haired animals such as mules and cattle also required less preparation for the show ring. Exhibitors used clippers to remove errant hair from ears, tails, and anywhere else that detracted from the animals' appearance. They then sprayed the animals' hair and hooves.

One of the difficulties in transporting animals to the fair was to get them to eat and drink adequately. The change from farm pasture or pen to fair pen or stall inevitably meant disruption in familiar routine, a change in the taste of water, and the excitement of being close to other strange animals. The taste of feed was less of a problem than that of water since usually we brought our own rations from the farm. Despite all our efforts, other circumstances often conspired to put the animals off their feed and drink.

Cows and sheep, more than the other animals, showed the result of this discombobulation, probably because of the multiple stomachs of these ruminants that quickly became slack. With pigs and mules a missed meal was less apparent. In order to show a cow or a lamb with a decently filled stomach, various techniques were used. The most common and benign one was to feed animals dried sugar beet pulp that had been soaked in water. The soaked pulp proved appetizing because of its sweetness, and animals ate it with relish. Once eaten, it expanded inside the digestive tract, filling out the animal's flanks with its considerable bulk. If enough were eaten, the animal's sides became plump and full.

There was, however, one drawback to the use of beet pulp: it was a powerful laxative, a kind of animal Metamucil. Fed the night before a morning exhibit, it worked well. After show time, the cow, less often the sheep, had loose stools, a fact that led to one event that remains in my memory to this day.

4-H members showing animals at fairs often experienced extreme boredom when tending their livestock in the barns. Accustomed to considerable physical activity, they now only had to feed and water their animals, clean out the manure, and keep the aisles swept clean or less spotted with debris. Their main outlet was talking with others, bragging about their animals, and scuffling or playing tricks on one another. If girls were present, boys enjoyed showing off with tricks designed to be funny and attract attention since they lacked the social skills to have any serious conversation with the opposite sex. I remember one boy who took a pair of his clean overalls and put it over his cow's rear end with the cow's hind legs in the overall legs. As he held the top of the overalls up over the rear, the cow defecated, spraying a loose stool all over the overalls and then over the startled boy who had dropped them. He then had to clean up the mess, not an easy job as his clean clothes were in the distant dorm. He succeeded in attracting attention but not, perhaps, the kind he wanted.

The cosmetic efforts of 4-H members to prepare their animals for showing paled beside the preparations of those who specialized in showing purebred stock. Some individuals went to great lengths to conceal the defects in their show animals. The insertion of wax or paraffin under an animal's skin to conceal a low vertebra was not uncommon. I also heard a tale about the bush of a cow's tail that had been frozen and had dropped off, and at the show was replaced with an artificial one.

Winning in any case was not easy. Even with an excellent animal, other factors often combined to deny the coveted blue or purple ribbon. One factor was changing fashions in the types of animals considered best, sometimes resulting from market preferences. Two examples will suffice.

In my pig project I raised and showed two breeds, Berkshire and Poland China hogs. Berkshires were a smaller, compact breed, short-bodied with plump hams and shoulders. The breed was relatively fat with a body that weighed 200 to 210 pounds at its optimum finish. At the time, however, bacon-type hogs were becoming more desirable. These were larger hogs with longer sides and bigger bodies that provided more bacon when slaughtered. As these became more popular, fears about eating fat grew, so the ideal hog became a long, lanky one whose meat contained less and less fat. Now the wheel has turned again, and gourmet chefs extol the flavor of the meat of Berkshire hogs that have more fat. The breed has regained popularity.

In the market lamb project, the same shifting of types also was evident. When I grew up the ideal market lamb was probably a Southdown, a compact, small animal that would be market ready at eighty to eighty-five pounds. One of my sister's champion lambs, a Shropshire-Southdown cross, weighed seventy-eight pounds. In the 1940s that ideal still ruled. Late in that era I showed a pen of Shropshire lambs at the International Livestock Exposition in Chicago. I did not win, but the winners were a pen of Southdowns, exhibited by the University of Kentucky, which could not have weighed more than eighty pounds each.

Yet the trend to larger animals could already be discerned. When I showed my lambs, few winners weighed more than 90 to 95 pounds. But Suffolk lambs weighing over 100 pounds were becoming more common in the competition. Today they dominate the market lamb classes, weighing 120 to 125 pounds. Small Shropshires and Southdowns grew less popular as breeders began emphasizing larger sheep in those breeds to meet the new competition. Thus, in order to win at exhibitions, Shropshire owners had to shift their flocks by selecting individual animals that conformed to the newer emphasis.

Another factor leading to uncertainty in the show ring involved the very nature of judging. I learned at an early age the great diversity of opinion that seems to characterize human choice. Most of the animals in any class were much like the women in beauty contests: all were excellent specimens and any of them might easily be rated tops. Despite their similarities, the judge had to rank them in some kind of order and then justify his selection. To do so he would usually emphasize certain features that appealed to him or could be easily recognized by others.

Emphasis upon certain features, however, did not explain the totality of a specimen. Sometimes the attitude of almost identical animals—a look in the eyes, a posture, an alertness, or just a general impression—made the difference.

A judge would be hard put to verbalize these differences and as a consequence would rely on more concrete, visible attributes.

This could get him into trouble. One year when I was showing sheep at the county fair, the judge felt the loin and the leg of the lamb, but he also felt the stub of the docked tail and commented on its shape and fatness. Sitting near the show ring, my grandfather, who never was shy about expressing his opinion, asked the judge in a loud voice if that was the part he ate.

To further complicate the matter, judges could forget or change their criteria for selecting a winner. One year the judge placed my market pigs low in the class because their pasterns were too sloping. (The pastern is the bone between the fetlock and the hoof.) The next year we made certain to show only pigs with less sloping pasterns—but the judge never even mentioned pasterns in his reasoning for placement. I lost again.

In general I came to believe that winning at the fair was as much a matter of chance as of the quality of the entry, and that outward appearance might be more important than the underlying excellence of the animal. I did not believe the judges were necessarily wrong. Indeed, when their opinions matched mine, I thought they were quite astute. These lessons were valuable and made my 4-H membership worthwhile.

Attendance at the fairs gave me more than just the experience of winning or losing. The Iowa State Fair in particular was a major social event for me as I spent the days away from home living in the boys' dorm there. Our family rarely traveled or stayed anywhere overnight while I was growing up. (We did not need to because our extended family lived so close by.) Coming to the fair gave me the opportunity to meet new people and learn new things. In the dorm some of that learning may have been suspect, and the mixing of boys aged ten to twenty-one certainly could produce trouble—fighting, bullying, and so forth. I do not remember much of that; I do remember debates over the relative attractiveness to girls of Aqua Velva and Old Spice aftershave. I particularly remember nights in those pre-television days when Herb Plambeck, the agricultural reporter for **WHO**, the major radio station in Iowa, read chapters of "The Most Dangerous Game" as we lay in our beds after lights out. It was a camping experience for one who never had been to camp.

The sheep barn and its inhabitants ultimately became familiar and welcoming to me. I made friends whom I kept for many years. Ike and Chet Ryan and I usually had a good time at the wrong (losing) end of the class. They told me when the watermelon feed was scheduled and about the graffiti in the men's toilet. I met other boys from other places and felt a sense of common endeavor.

Although I never became a farmer, the ideals if not the practice of 4-H helped me face the world with less fear and naiveté. Yet those ideals were often more implicit than explicit. Could one meet these goals even if one were not a farmer?

Similarly, my experience with **FFA** was important to me even if I did not go to an FFA fair or become a farmer. I did learn the use of certain tools and skills that served me in later life. My four years of FFA taught me, as the ten years of 4-H had, that there was more to farming than I had learned elsewhere, and that gaining this knowledge required effort and insight.

WINTER

*A winter chore: shoveling manure into
a manure spreader to be taken to the fields.*

WHEN DID WINTER COME? It seemed to descend around Thanksgiving and last through February. The snow often came as early as late November as the weather turned cold. I dreaded the cold and rarely felt warm until spring.

Preparation for winter began before the onset of the season. I had gotten my school clothes in September; among these were usually a new pair of overalls and a new pair of galoshes, the four-buckle kind. (Somehow the buckles rarely lasted more than a season.) If I had outgrown my shoes, I received a new pair of high-top work shoes. In the later thirties I also would have gotten a pair of felt inserts for galoshes that would cover several pairs of woolen socks. The inserts proved effective for keeping my feet warm during days of walking on frozen ground. Not every season but irregularly I would get either a sheepskin coat or a mackinaw. The sheepskin had a fleece lining and collar, with a canvas outer shell. It was utilitarian and could take hard use; it was not a fancy dress coat as today's can be. The canvas might be ripped and torn by protruding nails or pieces of wood jutting out from unexpected places. The mackinaw was usually wool and more likely to be worn on dressy occasions.

Hats, scarves, and mittens (rarely gloves) often came as gifts on my birthday or Christmas. Sometimes they were hand-me-downs. When Uncle Morris died, I inherited his old caps, which resembled those worn by streetcar conductors of an earlier time, and I was always embarrassed to be seen with them—I would start to school wearing one but would take it off en route so that I would arrive bareheaded. As a consequence I froze my ears; they have been tender and sensitive to cold weather ever since.

As we prepared our clothes, so we prepared the house for winter. The cast-iron stove that heated our dining room had been stored in a hall closet during the summer. We slid it out and placed it on a square metal pad, removed the round tin cover over the stovepipe hole in the wall, and inserted the pipe connecting the stove to the chimney. As I remember, we never cleaned the chimney, though we did the stovepipes. The soot in the chimney did catch fire once after I left home.

For fuel for the stove over the long winter we had accumulated coal and wood. Coal was not the most economical source of energy. Even though it was extremely cheap, it could not compete in price with wood we harvested ourselves. The farm had a woodlot of maples, ash, walnut, and butternut. Previous owners had evidently used the area for hogs or cattle to roam since the trees bordering the edge of the patch had pieces of barbed wire embedded in them. Father also allowed our hogs and cows to pasture there without the fence, to control the weeds and undergrowth.

During the course of the year, storms, particularly those with high winds, caused the trees to shed limbs or be blown completely over. Maples, the soft variety, were quite vulnerable and always dropped branches. Starting in the fall and continuing into the winter, our task was to process this fallen timber into usable stove wood. The wood needed to be dry; it was most suitable after the autumn rains had ended.

The harvesting of wood was labor intensive. If the tree was dead and still standing, it had to be cut down. Then the fallen tree had to be cut into manageable-size logs to be dragged near the house. Branches were trimmed with an axe, and the stripped log was cut into sections with a crosscut saw which required two persons to operate. (A one-person cross-cut existed, but our family did not have one.) Working a two-man saw was strenuous; the sawyers needed to share the same rhythm and resist exerting downward pressure on the saw. Novices often mistakenly tried to push the saw faster and would cause it to bind or drag through the wood.

Once cut into logs and hauled near the house, the wood was sawed into chunks some twelve to sixteen inches long by a rotary saw powered at first by a gasoline engine—the same one that Mother used to power the washing machine. Both the saw and the washing machine had pulleys connected by a belt to a pulley on the engine. After Father bought his own tractor, he used it to saw wood, replacing the gasoline engine.

To this point the wood was still not small enough to fit in the firebox of either stove; it had to be split into kindling along with sections of the larger branches that did not need sawing. Splitting was quite often my task, either on weekends or school holidays such as Thanksgiving and Christmas. The job was not onerous since the wood, especially the walnut and maple, had straight grains that split easily when struck squarely with an axe. The pieces that became firewood were consequently quite beautiful—straight and of wonderful color. I thought then, and even more now, that it was a shame to feed those strips into the stove.

Cutting up the wood called for considerable physical effort, and that always warmed me in the winter. I would have to remove a layer or two of clothing in order to have more freedom of motion and not become overheated. Even so, cutting wood always resulted in a sweaty body.

The summer and fall harvests usually provided enough animal feed to last until the following spring since in the warmer months the grass in the pasture replaced the grain and hay. That meant less feeding work and hauling of manure. But in winter the animals had to be fed and watered, the cows milked, and the horses harnessed and driven. These were tasks that had to be done every day, holidays included, and were finished before and after leaving for school.

The daily routine was almost always the same. My father would awaken me at five or five-thirty to do the morning chores. I would descend the stairs in my flannel pajamas to dress behind the dining room stove, shivering until I put on my long winter underwear and my first layer of clothes (a long-sleeve cotton or wool flannel shirt and denim overalls, not jeans). The myth that farm children were sewed into their underwear at the beginning of winter and cut out in the spring was just that, a myth. No one I knew had that done, but they, like me, changed their underwear infrequently. I put on a clean pair at least every week. For special occasions I would change more often.

Having fully dressed with my sheepskin coat and galoshes, I would go to the barn with my father by the light of a kerosene lantern—until 1937 when the farm was electrified. It was, of course, pitch-dark. After hanging the light on a nail in the barn, my father first lit the nearby water-tank heater to thaw the ice and warm the water for the livestock to drink.

In the winter, after the feeder lambs had gone to market, just one well and one tank sufficed for the remaining livestock. A concrete tank that contained a simple, cast-iron heater consisting of a firebox and chimney became the sole source for animal drinking water. The horses, sheep, and cattle drank from this tank while the hogs were supplied by buckets carried by hand.

The tank heater burned a variety of fuels—coal, wood, or often ears of spoiled corn and dry corncobs. (The recent substitution of the term "cob" for an ear of corn in cooking recipes would have been completely unfamiliar and confusing at that time.) Corn and cobs became the fuel of choice because they were convenient and cheaper than coal. And they made a hot fire.

The ears of corn burned in the heater were ears spoiled by mold or fungus and thus unsuitable for animal consumption. The reason for the spoilage lay in the method of harvesting and storage. Farmers might begin picking corn in October and not finish until December. Meanwhile the corn stored in the crib contained varying degrees of moisture, with the earliest harvest having the highest content and being most susceptible to mold and rot if not dried. There were few, if any, grain dryers at a time when most farms were without electricity or natural gas.

In order to allow the corn to dry, most corncribs were narrow and long with open spaces between the siding. This arrangement allowed, with varying degrees of success, the wind to blow through to dry the corn. It also encouraged rodents and birds to eat the crop. Exposure of the outer layer of corn to the elements led to further spoilage. The upshot was that the rotten ears had to be sorted out before feeding corn to the animals, providing an ample supply of fuel for the tank heater.

After starting the fire in the heater, father and I drove the cows into the barn to milk by lantern light. If it was not terribly cold, they had been in the pasture; otherwise they had been in the barn's shelter, next to the cattle stalls. They would be eager to come in because they were hungry and because their distended udders hurt. The cleated plank outside that served as their entry to the stalls might be snow covered and icy, so they would walk in gingerly. If they had been outside, snow or ice might also cover their backs.

Although the barn was unheated and had many gaps in its siding, it was warmer than outside because of the animal heat, because of the hay in the loft that provided insulation, and because of shelter from the wind. The cows' hides began to steam as they warmed up and as we prepared to milk them. Because of the cold weather, the damp teats were often chapped or cracked and needed to be soothed with Bag Balm. One advantage of rubbing on the lotion was that it warmed our cold hands and prevented the cows from kicking or resisting milking. It also helped our chapped and cracked hands. Milking was not an unpleasant task in winter; I preferred doing it in that season despite the possibility of being hit in the face by a frozen, mud-encrusted tail. It usually took thirty to forty-five minutes. As I pulled at the teats (we always milked by hand), I kept my head in the cow's flank to avoid the tail and to help prevent the animal from kicking. My cap usually became covered with cow hairs.

From the four to five cows we usually milked, we carried the milk to the house. We put the two horses in the barn if we planned to use them that day. We also checked the sheep and hogs and fed them if the sun was up. In the house I usually hand-turned the separator that separated the cream from the milk. The skim milk went to feed the hogs or calves while the cream went into a five-gallon can that we took to a local creamery once a week. My mother saved enough whole milk for the family to drink, as she and my father looked with scorn on our nearby neighbors who fed their children skim or "blue" milk. She also reserved enough cream for our cereal and to churn our own sweet cream butter. We had enough cream in the summer to make ice cream, but we never made it in winter though we did add snow to milk and cream to make an inferior substitute.

After eating breakfast, which usually consisted of eggs and meat (ham or bacon or sausage, all homemade) as well as the ever-present oatmeal that my father insisted upon, I helped finish the animal feeding and was off to school. Sometimes I changed clothes if I had gotten them too dirty, and I tried to clean the manure and spilled milk off my shoes or galoshes.

Bloomfield School was two miles distant, and classes began at 9 a.m. We walked to school most of the time in winter as we had in the spring and fall. If it was raining or snowing too hard, my father or neighbor with school-age children drove us in their cars to and from school. Once my father came in the middle of a blizzard with a team and wagon to take us home because the roads had drifted shut, an event that evoked much comment at the time and remains firmly fixed in my memory to this day.

That was unusual. Mostly we walked; and, because it was winter, we frequently started just as the sun was rising. Excused from school at 4 p.m., we arrived home as the sun was setting. If it was cloudy, as it frequently was in winter, the walks were cold and gloomy.

Arriving in school, I knew I would be warm again, perhaps too warm, since the large classroom contained a cast-iron stove that was really hot. The amount of heat you received, however, depended upon your distance from the stove. If you were quite close, you were too hot; if you were far away in a corner, you might be too cold. That affected what and how many clothes to wear to school. There had to be enough layers for the two-mile walk but, at the same time, not too many or too difficult to remove in order to adjust to the temperature of the schoolroom.

The uneven heat exacerbated the problem of smelliness. Most of the students took baths infrequently and smelled bad. What's more, the soft coal used in the stove burned with a sulfurous smell, and other noxious odors were common in the closed room.

We could escape the smell during recess (two during the day, mid-morning and mid-afternoon) or at lunch, weather permitting. If not, we were confined all day without escape. If the weather allowed and if there was snow on the ground, we could play "fox and geese" or throw snowballs or build snowmen. There was, however, no place to sit except on the ground. We had to return inside to a smelly, overheated room to eat our lunch.

Where I ate mattered little to me, for I was always hungry. Exercise and cold winter air honed my appetite even for the cold meat sandwiches my mother made and I carried in a brown paper bag from elementary school through high school. I remember envying my fellow students who had bologna or cheese sandwiches while I had only beef or pork. If I had a cookie or cake, they were also homemade.

When I got home from school I would again be ravenous and would usually have a snack before going out to do the evening chores, which repeated those in the morning. Then I would eat supper and read lying down behind the stove by the light of a kerosene lamp. I do not remember listening to the radio until electrification, though I remember a large battery-powered unit in a storage room. When we did buy an electric radio, I listened mostly to the radio station from Iowa State College. It was much favored by my father and grandfather because it broadcast primarily farm market reports and household hints along with news and classical music. The last made a permanent impression on me, perhaps because it was the first programmed music I heard. The radio was the sole source for music until we bought a piano for my sisters to play.

Winter found me less busy with outside work because I was in school most of the day. But on weekends or school holidays I was available for necessary tasks.

Besides the daily chores, the work mainly involved spreading the manure that had accumulated in the summer and fall. In those busier times, other, more pressing tasks had crowded out the disposition of manure. Consequently the droppings from horses and cows had been thrown in piles just adjacent to the barn. The piles had grown into substantial deposits that, while frozen and often snow-covered on top, were sometimes still warm and fermenting inside. The manure had to be removed in warmer periods when the exterior had thawed somewhat.

This arrangement was not the case with the feces of feeder sheep bought in the fall. As they roamed the cornfields and the pasture, they spread their droppings in a fairly even way over those fields. But in the one barn devoted to providing shelter and hay to the sheep in rainy and snowy weather, the manure deposit was another matter. As the sheep came into the barn to eat or to get out of the inclement weather, they packed the dirt floor with mud from their feet and their own feces and then pulled the hay out of the mangers that they also trampled. With five hundred sheep packed together in the barn, the deposits mounted up. By the time we sold the sheep, the mixture of mud, hay, and manure reached one to two feet above the original floor level, to become almost even with the feeders.

Besides the slackening of other work pressure, the winter season was the best time to spread the manure for other reasons. In the first place, the manure spreader did not compact the soil as it could and did in the muddy spring and fall. Second, the manure slowly leached into the soil as the ground thawed and thus would not "burn" or overfertilize the next year's crop. A final and less compelling reason was that removal emptied the deposit areas so they could be refilled the following year.

I didn't mind the job. The piles of horse and cow manure were easy to fork except for the frozen sections on top. Cow manure had more frozen segments since it contained more liquid than the drier horse manure. On the other hand, the pounding of hundreds of small hooves in the sheep barn had made a fibrous mat that was extremely difficult to pull apart. The uprooting required considerable prying and teasing to carve out pieces small enough for the spreader.

For spreading the manure, the horses had to be harnessed and hitched to the spreader. Made frisky by the cold, they resisted at first, especially at being bridled since that bit of harness went over the head and ears. One of a pair of mules that Grandfather had given us to train and use had evidently been beaten around the head and consequently bobbed his head strenuously to avoid being bridled. He also was the one that had killed a man by crushing him against the stall, so he needed to be approached cautiously. Even the gentlest of horses hated to have the cold bit put into their mouth and slobbered in copious streams as they chewed at the frigid metal.

Once hitched to the spreader the horses settled down, and the work of loading and unloading began. Neither was difficult for the horses. Spreading evenly was easy as the pieces of manure previously spread could be seen on the frozen ground or in the snow, marking a driving path. Still, there were unpleasant aspects. Gripping the reins to control the horses pulling a relatively light load soon resulted in cramped and numb fingers because of the cold. And because of the design of the spreader, it was not uncommon to be hit in the back with lumps of frozen manure.

As I grew older I sometimes earned money by hiring out to other farmers when I was not needed at home. I remember one such occasion when my Uncle Frank decided he could use extra help and hired me, offering me a unique experience. Uncle Frank liked to combine experiments with recent developments in farming and older, mostly abandoned practices. He kept bees, grew exotic melons in his cornfield, and raised other crops unfamiliar to us, such as different kinds of sorghums.

One of his practices that was pretty much of a relic was the reason for my employment. Uncle Frank had cut the cornstalks by hand in one field, shocked them earlier in the fall, and now wanted to haul the stalks into the barn to feed his substantial dairy herd. I knew what corn shocks were from pictures of Halloween but had rarely seen them in anyone's field. The dried-out stalks (called stover) had little value as feed except for their remaining ears of corn, for the dead leaves had lost just about every nutrient but fiber. Most farmers either burned the stalks after picking the corn in the fall or disked the fields in the spring to cut up the stalks, then plowed the residue under for fertilizer before planting another crop.

My days helping out with the stover usually followed this schedule. I arrived at my uncle's farm about 7:30 a.m. after helping with morning chores at home and eating breakfast at 6 a.m. We began work soon after the sun rose. We drove a hayrack to the field where the three of us—I, my uncle, and my cousin—cut the twine on the shocks, loaded the separated stalks, drove to the barn, and unloaded the hayrack, all in about an hour. We worked hard and fast. My uncle was a workaholic who often ran from one task to another in his impatience to get work done, and usually wanted to make another trip after completing four round-trips in the morning. It was now noon, and I was starving because breakfast had been six hours earlier and because of the appetite I had gained from the cold weather and the exercise. But Uncle

Frank insisted, and we made another run for more stalks, stopping for dinner at about 1 p.m.

My aunt Rosina, however, knowing my uncle's habits quite well, had not even begun to prepare the noon meal. I suppose she thought he might decide to go for still another load. In any case, we waited in the house for at least an hour while she cooked a large and sumptuous dinner. The wonderful aroma of her cooking only increased my hunger, and when we finally sat down to eat I stuffed myself with heavy farm food (my aunt was an excellent cook). Having finished the meal, my uncle now announced that we should return to work since we had had our rest before we ate. My stomach hurt for the next hour, not from being too empty but from being too full. We worked for another three hours or until it began to get dark. Then I went home to help with the evening chores. No wonder I was happy to return to school after winter vacation ended.

Outside of these experiences, I did not work in the cold all that much in the winter. This was because of the kind of work to be done in that season, and because my parents worried about my health. I suffered from pleurisy, and my breathing of frigid air aggravated it. I also had frequent colds. Since my father believed in the efficacy of chiropractic, I often traveled to Oskaloosa for treatment, so memories of winter cold are inextricably connected with painful spinal adjustments in a rather gloomy second-floor office on cloudy, cold days.

Not all winter work had to be done outside in the worst weather. Some could be moved inside, most of it concerning preparation for the next planting season. Nursery and seed catalogs occupied most of Father's interior time. A great lover of trees, he read descriptions of fruit and nut trees that portrayed the luscious produce of these wonderful saplings that never quite met expectations. Most of the mail orders he sent were for trees to be planted when the ground thawed. He did not order vegetable seeds or plants by mail; these came from local vendors.

Until the hybridization of corn became more common among Iowa farmers in the 1930s, my father used selected seed corn from previous harvests for the next year's planting. He visited his corncrib and selected the best corn specimens. (He was a prizewinning judge of corn and grain.) He would take a few kernels from those ears, wrap them in a bit of damp cloth, and place them near the heating stove in order to keep them warm. At regular intervals he would unwrap the cloths and inspect the seeds to determine how many had sprouted as well as their size and presumed strength. He would then select the ears containing the best kernels. These ears went into a hand-cranked sheller until he had enough for planting. He even extended this practice to hybrid corn. After purchasing enough seed for one season's crop, he would not buy the second year's seed but would select it from the first year's harvest. While hybrid seed corn producers frowned on the practice, claiming that the second crop lacked the strength and vigor of the original seed, the results were equivocal and the practice more economical. It soon ended as we, like other farmers, grew accustomed to buying hybrid seed corn every year.

Father did not usually buy chemical fertilizer for the crops. If he was growing alfalfa, he might plan to spread lime to make the soil less acid. If he was planting soybeans or alfalfa, he would add a bacterial fix to the seed to help with the nitrogen-fixing ability of the crop. That was the extent of his chemical usage until after World War II when he began to apply a nitrogen dressing on corn.

But life in winter had play as well as work. It was the season with the two special holidays, Thanksgiving and Christmas. Thanksgiving was celebrated by our nuclear family, but

Christmas involved our extended clan. While we exchanged gifts and had a feast at home, either on Christmas Eve or Christmas Day, we also celebrated with another gift exchange and feast with my grandfather and grandmother, uncles and aunts, and cousins. By the mid-1930s, that group alone numbered at least twenty-two. Sometimes relatives of my aunts also came and added to the total.

The location of the family get-together rotated through a six-year cycle, and the pattern remained pretty much the same. The host family provided the meat, quite often chicken or turkey, while the guest families brought other food—casseroles, salads, desserts, and side dishes. Quantities of nuts were always on hand, unshelled with nutcrackers, and hard candy. Everyone overate, causing a few participants to lie on the floor or on a couch and snooze after stuffing themselves.

When we exchanged gifts in the depression years, their maximum value was one dollar. Each of us drew one name from all the family members so that everyone received at least one gift. The children often got more, however, particularly from our grandparents or our childless uncle and aunt. These were often utilitarian—warm mittens, scarves, and so forth—but sometimes they were books or toys.

After eating and naps, the men went outdoors to look at the farm buildings and animals or other aspects of the host's enterprise. At least partially recovered from the food in the cold air, we took the opportunity to urinate outside. It was still a rural custom for men to relieve themselves outdoors, not in an outhouse but in a stall, up against a building, or behind a tree. It wasn't so much a lack of facilities as it was a preference for the outdoors and a kind of tribal ritual.

These Christmas festivities had been preceded by the holiday program at school, marking the start of the two-week vacation. Part of the expectation of the school's trustees was that the teacher direct a program showing off the pupils' musical or dramatic talents. I reflect now on how difficult it must have been for Miss Anderson to stage a decent production with so little equipment and so little talent among the students. Before electrification the only musical instrument the school owned was a mechanical phonograph wound by hand and a number of rather scratchy records. Lighting came from white gas lamps or Coleman lanterns. The stage consisted of a small, elevated platform at the front of the schoolhouse that lacked a curtain. The program included both musical and spoken acts, a kind of variety show. I remember one such program where I sang a duet with a girl my age. The song was "When You and I Were Young, Maggie," the musing of an octogenarian couple reflecting on a long-lost youth. I can imagine how that appeared to the audience since I was (and still am) tone deaf, and all of ten years old.

On one occasion the school's program shifted its locale from the schoolhouse to the Friends Church across the road. The reason for the move remains unclear—more room for the audience, perhaps a larger stage. In any case, I remember that a number of us paraded to "The March of the Wooden Soldiers," stamping our feet in a mostly disorganized drill. And we had the tallest Christmas tree I had ever seen to that time, lighted by candles. Even more astonishing to me now is that there seemed to be no particular concrn about, or provision for, fire.

My family always had a Christmas tree cut from a small plot of evergreens that served as a windbreak next to one of our barns. These red cedar firs made poor Christmas trees, scraggly with few branches and lacking the aroma or shapeliness of today's trees. We had no candles on the tree; it remained unlighted until electricity made lights possible.

After Christmas, no holidays provided a break from the usual work routine. We never celebrated Lincoln's Birthday, Valentine's Day, Washington's Birthday, St. Patrick's Day, Easter, or Memorial Day. Weather brought change: the snow provided a break in routine. We could go sledding when that happened, though the Iowa hills were not steep enough to make for the most thrilling rides; and the new snow often was either too wet or too dry to provide the best and fastest sliding.

It was the big snow of 1936 that proved most novel. It snowed and snowed, piling up so high that the secondary roads remained unplowed and impassable for a week or more. Only the primary highway running by our farm was open. As a consequence, three of my uncles walked over the fields to ride into town with us to buy the supplies necessary for their families. This was an exciting diversion.

The winter changed our shopping patterns too. We no longer went to town as much on Saturday night after a hard day's labor in the fields. Now we would go usually in the afternoon, before having to return home to do the chores. This schedule became even more normal after 1937 when we were involved in a fatal accident. Remorseful, my father very much disliked driving after dark or in inclement weather.

The accident occurred on a dark winter's night on a slippery highway. Iowa highways had a peculiar feature that constituted a driving hazard. The roads had a raised, curving edge that supposedly directed water from the road itself to drains placed at lower levels. But if a driver swerved and ran up on the ridged edge, he had a tendency to oversteer, and on a wet or icy road this might result in a skid and an accident. A man returning from Des Moines did exactly that one Saturday night when we were on the way to town with Father driving, our hired man in the front seat, and my sister and I in the rear. His approaching car skidded in front of us. My father attempted to go around to the left to avoid the oncoming car but struck the rear end instead. A woman passenger in the rear seat hit her head on a window frame, suffered a concussion, and died a week later. The scene remains indelible in my mind as I am certain it did in my father's until the day of his death.

I was happy to see winter end, when the weather grew warmer, we were less isolated, and I felt healthier. Still I missed the cloudless days when the snow had not yet turned grey from soot or dust, and the cold clear nights, with the aurora borealis visible in the northern sky, when the stars with no intervening light seemed close enough to touch.

A typical Iowa farmstead in the 1930s, before rural electrification.
A windcharger provided low-wattage power.

Sunset: Why I Am Not a Farmer

☙ I STILL HAVE a recurrent dream, though now it occurs more and more rarely. I am alone in a large two-story white farmhouse, gripped with a sense of anxiety and foreboding. Although I have seen the house but once, I recognize it immediately. I am older, probably in my fifties, unmarried and without prospects for marriage or for other employment. I feel desperate, but I do not know why. Then I wake up without any resolution or explanation of that dream.

Once awake, I think I know what anxiety the dream, or nightmare, reflects. The clue is the house.

Late in the 1940s, after I had finished college but had not yet decided upon a future, my father found a farm to buy that he suggested would be large enough to provide a good living for both him and me. It was located some twenty-five miles east of us, south of Sigourney, a small Iowa town, with several hundred acres of bottomland and a big modern house with electricity and running water and four bedrooms. We drove over one day to view the farmstead. This was the house that appears in my dream.

World War II had ended the depression for farmers that had begun after World War I. My father had become more prosperous; he had paid off the loan on the farm and had purchased a new car to replace the twelve-year-old used Chevrolet he had been driving. Prices for farm products had risen, and it appeared they would remain high. Nations recovering from the war needed the food American farms produced.

I was reluctant to agree to my father's proposition but, as usual, was of mixed feelings about it. I agonized over the decision and felt considerable relief when my mother refused to move. She rejected buying the new place mainly because of my younger sister Helen who was near high school age. Mother believed that Helen would have to attend a high school that was inferior to Oskaloosa High School and perhaps even be denied the opportunity to attend college as my sister Alice and I had.

Her decision puzzled me at the time, and still does. She had grown up in an even smaller community, Deep River, than Sigourney and had attended a smaller high school. I do know she was quite often lonely and missed her relatives who lived some distance away. She also resented my grandfather, who dominated my father, gave my mother unwanted advice, and treated our house as his own, walking in unannounced. I thought she might welcome an escape from him and an opportunity to live in a much nicer home. But I was wrong.

Left up to me, the decision would have been difficult. Life on the farm still attracted me greatly; even now, I look back with nostalgia and sometimes regret for not having chosen that path. I believe my dream reflects the hidden fear that helped me support my mother's wishes. I think it encapsulates one element of that fear, the element of social isolation.

I was in my early twenties when I first had this dream. I had no girlfriend nor had I ever had one in high school or college. I feared I would never have one. My chances seemed even more slender in the greater rural isolation of the proposed purchase. I had no desire to become a bachelor farmer like those I had known when growing up—the butt of jokes and sometimes pity.

My network of relatives that had given me emotional support seemed to be dissolving. Uncle Carl and his family had sold their farm and moved north to a larger, more level, and more fertile farm near New Sharon. Dale, one of my four male cousins, now studied agriculture at Iowa State, and I had lost touch with him. Lyle, Uncle Dick's only son, was in college at Monmouth while Herbert, Uncle Frank's only son, was in a federal penitentiary in Missouri, serving a sentence for draft resistance.

My older sister Alice worked in a public library in Ottumwa; only my younger sister Helen lived at home. My grandfather and grandmother were both in their eighties, and my grandmother seemed increasingly frail. My father was nearly sixty years old but was in better health than my mother, who suffered from high blood sugar and an irregular heartbeat.

I did not know then how soon my extended family would disintegrate. My grandfather and grandmother both died about two years later. He had been the center around whom the family rotated, and his death marked the loosening of the bonds that held it together. Soon came the near dissolution of the Hoover compound that consisted of four farms— my grandfather's and those of his three sons—adjoining one another. At a private auction limited to family members, Uncle Frank outbid Uncle Freeman for Grandfather's remaining land (Grandfather had sold forty acres to Uncle Dick just before he died). Uncle Freeman sold his farm soon after and moved to New Mexico; Uncle Frank moved to his new purchase. Neither Lyle nor Dale became farmers; and when Uncle Frank and Uncle Dick died, no Hoover held land in what had been a Hoover enclave.

Even without any foreknowledge, I knew that family relationships would be affected by the move my father contemplated. He had always relied on my grandfather for guidance; he was, even at age sixty, still quite dependent on his father to help make decisions. Away from the region as we would be, we would no longer receive Grandfather's almost daily visits and probably would not make our Sunday trips to his house. Father would be more on his own.

That aloneness would make not only for more psychological and emotional solitude but also for an absence of available labor in crucial farmwork times. We still needed help putting up hay, and our own sheep operation could not have continued as easily without uncles to help vaccinate, sort, and load the animals. Even a farm that had no livestock would require extra help in harvesting, someone to drive the wagon or truck up to the combine-harvester to empty the grain hopper—unless, of course, that help was a hired worker.

After World War II, more people were doing custom (hired) farmwork. Some were GIs who invested the money saved from their service in new equipment that had now become more plentiful. The farmer who hired the work done saved the cost of buying the machines, but the situation had obvious drawbacks. Custom workers with equipment preferred to hire out for large acreages. Often they scheduled the cutting of smaller ones at times that did not harvest the grain at its optimum ripeness. Sometimes these machines were not even available during harvest season.

While the war's end had meant a greater availability of labor-saving equipment and their operators, it had not expanded the pool of individuals willing to work as hired men.

The depression years always saw a labor surplus made up of men who would eagerly take such jobs in order to survive. Most were young single men who hoped to work in this position long enough to save money to become tenant farmers, with an ultimate goal of becoming farm owners. Both Uncle Freeman and Uncle Carl had live-in hired men before the war, but none after. We too employed temporary help (for a few days or weeks) in prewar days, but none after. That source of itinerant labor had vanished with the availability of other jobs or with the federal aid given to returning veterans to enter educational and training programs.

The remaining source of labor in times of harvest could be one's neighbors. From earlier times, a long tradition of aid in a period of grief survived in most rural communities. If one's husband or son had died, neighbors came with their equipment to pick corn or put up hay. But this tradition could be found chiefly in older, more settled communities where neighbors had known one another for a long time. Even then they helped only in extraordinary circumstances. If we moved into the new farm, it was not a given that we could count on such aid.

My waning sense of community with my relatives was not my only concern. The great emotional problem was my relationship with my father and the question of whether I could break free from him to assert my independence. I had come to recognize how he leaned upon his own father; would I repeat the experience with him? I knew that I lacked the aggressiveness of my grandfather, and I found my father to be a dominant figure. I still deeply respected and loved him, but could I manage to assert my opinions without confronting or hurting him?

Little did I know at the time what my parents' future would be. Diagnosed with coronary artery disease, my father would have to retire from strenuous physical work in fewer than five years. My mother's several illnesses resulted in her death not ten years later. If I had chosen to farm in a new area, I would soon have been the only farm operator, with a younger sister in school and a father of limited activity.

But I could not know about that vision of the future, nor would I allow my emotional state to determine my decision. After all, there were other farms in other places that might have met my mother's objections and still have kept us near our relatives. My decision to become a farmer rested mostly on two questions: Did I have the interest and ability to be a farmer? Were external circumstances such that farming would give me a good future, providing an adequate living and a happy life?

An honest assessment of my interests and abilities showed both strengths and weaknesses. On the plus side, I enjoyed physical work, even in rain or snow. But I sometimes found certain tasks monotonous. I particularly disliked swinging a scythe to cut weeds along fencerows in one-hundred-degree summer weather with high humidity; and I found ten to twelve hours on a tractor, plowing or cultivating, stultifying. But the variety of tasks that composed a farmer's year reduced that monotony and contributed to the development of different skills.

I particularly enjoyed working with animals and believed I had a talent for understanding them—at least that's what other people often said about me. I could distinguish between individuals even among the five hundred head of sheep that we fed for three months every fall. I had also come to believe that each animal had distinct characteristics that differentiated it from another, characteristics that in humans might be called personality. Once these had been identified, actions could be anticipated: which animal would stray from the flock, which horse was most timid and likely to spook when hearing an unusual sound or seeing an unexpected sight.

On the other hand, I shrank from those tasks that involved inflicting pain—castration, cutting off tails, and so forth—even to the point of disliking those actions that were merely discomforting to animals, such as worming and vaccinating. However much I rationalized that the practices protected the animal (though that didn't hold for castration), they nonetheless bothered me. The dread that caused me to flee when I was just ten years old, when my father asked me to hold a lamb while he castrated it and then docked it, remained.

Giving up raising animals and instead buying young ones that were already vaccinated and castrated could solve this dilemma fairly easily. We did that with our feeder lambs, and already corporations were advertising germ-free pigs that were feedlot ready. In an age of specialization, these companies could do a more efficient job, and a less expensive one, than a small producer. Yet with the convenience came limitations. The buyer would probably need to expand feeding facilities in order to compensate for the added cost of buying instead of raising the animals. And more waste would have to be disposed of in some fashion.

But the risk inherent in feeding out animals could be shared by contracting out the finishing of market animals to market processors who would feed and sell the fattened animals. This operation substituted corporate judgment for the farm operator's and led to a perceived loss of farmer independence. The contract system had already begun, particularly with chickens, and was expanding. It was almost certain to become more and more influential.

Despite my attraction for animal husbandry, I was no fan of feedlots and disliked working with animal waste. We avoided a good deal of that confinement by allowing the sheep to harvest the cornfields and run freely in the pasture. Thus the animals spread their own manure, which had a much less offensive odor than that of chickens, hogs, or cows, and which did not create a noxious mixture with mud that served as the feedlot base.

Beyond all these considerations, my major shortcoming in becoming a farmer was my lack of skill in machine operation and repair. Part of this ineptitude came from a lack of interest, part from a lack of instruction and practice. While I learned to drive both a tractor and a car when I was twelve, I never cared to explore their inner workings or the limits of their performance.

Because our first tractor belonged to three brothers and my father, he worried continually about it being damaged. Consequently he took it on himself to drive the tractor in difficult circumstances and to do both routine maintenance and necessary repairs. Nor did he take much time to instruct me in what exactly he was doing. I learned by watching him, but I rarely did the work myself.

Many farm tasks that involved machinery were seasonal and thus lacked the kind of repetition that led to familiarity and competence. How many times did the canvases need to be placed on the binder and adjusted? Once in a season if done properly. Each time the task needed to be done, my memory of the preceding year's procedures had been long lost.

Certain other jobs, such as changing oil and greasing, I mastered since they were simple and repetitive. But these were superficial skills and did not go to the heart of machine operation and repair.

While operating any mechanical device I had a great fear that I might break something. My fear certainly stemmed from a lack of self-confidence, but also from my father's concern over the consequences of such damage—which I think was in turn a product of his constant worry over having enough money to keep the farm. His insecurity fed into mine, especially when he cautioned me to be careful at times that I was trying my hardest to be so.

I knew that the machinery of the future would be even more complex and fear inspiring. This was already happening. Sensing a market demand for farm equipment, manufacturers were expanding at war's end by adding new features, increasing both the size and power of their tractors and stepping up their advertising. The early row-crop tractors now seem underpowered and dwarfish compared to the new models, as a visit to an antique tractor display today will attest.

But the increasing complexity in size and power demanded that enough land be cultivated to pay for the added cost of the next generation of machines. In order to stay solvent, then, a farmer must either become less competitive by relying on less powerful equipment or expand his cultivated land in order to enlarge his cash crop. Which came first, the expansion of the land area or the larger implements to farm it? Who could tell?

When World War II ended the farm depression, farmers had ready cash to pay for new equipment and buy additional land. The federal government's shift to a withholding tax on wages did not affect farmers as they remained on the older system of self-reporting. Not that many farmers before the war had earned enough to pay an income tax. I know my father did not; he began filing tax returns only in the war years. Many farmers were less ethical than he was. I heard farmers brag on the street at the time that they did not pay income taxes, nor did they plan to file returns.

Recently discharged veterans were also competing with established farm operators for available land. They had access to several federal programs that aided those who wished to return to the farm. Although not as well known as the GI Bill that enabled veterans to go to college, these programs provided educational grants for vocational training, which included agriculture, and loans to purchase farmsteads.

Buyer pressure forced the price of land higher, making our farm more valuable and allowing us a bigger pot of money to buy a larger acreage. How much that would have been I never knew. In our family the discussion of money and sex was prohibited except for my father's deploring his lack of funds. I did know that he now had more money since he had finally paid off the farm mortgage.

Because of my depression experience, I had a deep fear of falling into poverty. My father told me the same story over and over again about how he had been unable to meet the payments on a $1,000 life insurance policy he had taken out in his good years, and consequently had failed even to collect any cash value from it when it lapsed. When I was seven years old in 1933 and our local bank closed, I lost my small bank account consisting of money I had earned riding the hay horse. Later my father told me, when I asked him for the pennies I usually gave in Sunday school, then held in my grandparents' house, that he had no money to give me. To me that meant our family had none. Even now I become too focused on the cost of every item and often choose the cheaper rather than the better one.

I knew this attitude would serve me poorly as a farmer since it might prevent me from making necessary expenditures or cloud my judgment on farm planning and operation. We are all victims of our history; I am no exception.

But I was also a victim of my father's and grandfather's history as well. The period immediately following World War II resembled very much that after World War I. Farm prices remained high as the world demand for food continued strong. People had money to buy items that had been scarce, and in the United States at least there was an air of prosperity.

After World War I my grandfather had expanded by buying farmland in the Red River Valley, land he lost in the subsequent hard times that followed. It almost caused him to lose his home. My father and his brothers bought farms when land prices were high and had to struggle hard to keep them while scraping by for twenty years. My father thought about giving up his farm and going to work in the post office, and Uncle Carl told his son Dale that he would probably have been better off had he gone bankrupt and lost the farm.

Who could be sure these conditions would not return? The history of farming was replete with times of boom and bust, so why wouldn't the cycle repeat itself? That was my thinking at the time.

I did not wish to live in the same conditions of poverty and deprivation I had experienced—even though I realized that my experience was better than that of many of my generation. Being young, I accepted the idea that change was constant, but emotionally I still thought in terms of continuity. It was difficult to imagine a different future at a new farm, and I marveled that my father as he neared sixty would have the courage to begin a new venture.

So finally I would not have chosen to be a farmer, even had my mother agreed to move. In the near future my fears for American agriculture seemed to have been quite misplaced. The Korean War helped continue farm prosperity, as did the rest of the 1950s. (One great irony was that my Quaker grandfather and father, who were anti-war, found their greatest prosperity because of wars.) Had we purchased the farm, we too would have prospered in those times.

Yet this may have been only a short-term gain. The prosperity enjoyed by some did not come to others. As young farmers bought land, many took on debt they could not repay, and in ensuing decades they left the land for another job or vocation. My own cousin Herbert, the only cousin who became a farmer, lost the farm he inherited from his father in part because he modernized too fast. He bought the latest equipment and the most popular new breeds of animals but could not sustain his debt and went under.

If I had become a farmer, would that have happened to me, or would I have become a surviving success? I often wonder about that, and think I too would probably not have survived. If I had, I would most likely be living alone in the big house in my dream. But even that destiny would have had its compensations.

Reflection: I Was Not the Only One

> "Indeed, it's worth asking again; is there any
> cause to think a place—any place—within its
> plaster and joints, its trees and plantings, in its
> putative essence *ever* shelters some spirit ghost of
> us as proof of its significance and ours."
> —Richard Ford, *Independence Day*

✻ IN MY MIND'S EYE I remain an Iowa boy, proud of the state and with an outlook on life firmly shaped by a twenty-five-year immersion in rural and small-town life. I decided against farming in 1948 and entered a Ph.D. program at the University of Iowa in 1950. I began teaching outside the state in 1953 after receiving a degree in history. I never lived in Iowa again, though from time to time I visited my father and my sister Helen; and my middle daughter, Sara, graduated from the University of Iowa.

In the fall of 1993 I decided to return to Iowa for my fiftieth high school reunion. I had just retired after many years as a college professor and had time to reflect on the life I had led elsewhere and the life I could have led had I stayed on an Iowa farm. Although my wife and I had decided not to retire

189

in Iowa despite some emotional attachment on my part, I still hoped I could find elements of the past that would offer some insight into an alternate life, one not lived. This insight would come, I thought, from those of my age and even from the landscape itself. I was intrigued by the floods that had inundated parts of Iowa that spring and summer; mostly, though, it was curiosity about what had happened to my classmates and the farms I had known.

In late September I flew from Sarasota, Florida, where I now live, to Iowa. As the plane banked to land at St. Louis and again at Des Moines, the extent of the flood was all too evident. I mused on the reasons why the flood had so interested me. Was it because the weather was such an important element in farm life that it had assumed a permanent place in my psyche? (I still begin conversations with distant friends and relatives with inquiries about the weather.) Or was it because floods were such an important part of ancient myths that they had become part of the collective memory that Jung claimed we all shared? Did I subconsciously worry that the flood had swept away all markers of the past along with the memories they signified? Rationally I knew I should not worry about Oskaloosa, which sat on the high ground between the Des Moines and Skunk rivers. The Skunk was the source of the town's drinking water, a fact that never failed to amuse out-of-towners.

When I arrived in Des Moines it was still raining, but the water had receded from its highest levels and the city appeared quite normal. After renting a car and dining with friends I left for Oskaloosa, replicating the route chosen by Robert Kinkaid in *The Bridges of Madison County*, south on US 65 to Route 92. When I reached 92 I briefly thought of turning west to visit Winterset in Madison County. A former colleague owned a bank there, but the town had little to interest me. I had seen some of the covered bridges as well as the birthplace of John Wayne. George Washington Carver had stayed in the town before enrolling at Simpson College, but I was uncertain whether there was any trace of his stay. When I first read *The Bridges of Madison County* I was struck by the preposterous plot. What bothered me from the start was the device that the author, Robert James Waller, used to remove Francesca's husband and children from the farm. He had them going to the Illinois State Fair to show Carolyn's 4-H steer. The reason was obvious: the Iowa State Fair in Des Moines was too nearby for them to be out of the picture. But a 4-H steer would not be shown out of state; there would be no classes for it nor any rule allowing entry. That fact ruined any semblance of reality for me. But the novel might provide an insight into contemporary Iowa: war brides had added more ethnic diversity to the state, along with Latino laborers who worked in the packing plants.

The face of the land as I drove the some sixty miles east to Oskaloosa interested me. There were few fences and large barns; some farms had larger groups of animals—cattle or hogs—than the pastures I had known in my youth. The cropland had become predominantly monocultural with corn or soybeans, with longer contoured rows instead of smaller straight ones, and with grass planted in what had been erodible channels.

After a rainy drive I arrived at my motel, too late for the class picnic at the Friendship Inn on Friday evening. It continued to rain that night and the next morning as I drove to the Inn for the day's activities. When I entered the hospitality room, no one recognized me. I recognized a few of the men sitting on folding chairs around the sides of the room, which also contained tables of food—cheese, cold cuts, and rich desserts—none of which I was supposed to eat for reasons of health, as well as bottles of 7-Crown whiskey. Women were slightly in the majority. As I had witnessed in family gatherings as a boy and in similar groups at other times and places, the gathering was informally separated by gender, the women talking mainly to other women and the men to one another.

I recognized none of the women. Perhaps the failure was a product of my atypical high school experience. I was only twelve years old when I entered high school and was painfully shy. Besides, I was a farm boy, and at the time (1939) there was a wide gulf between those who lived on farms and those who lived in town. I had no social life in high school: no dates, no dances, no parties. I thought some of the girls were attractive, but I lacked the confidence to talk comfortably with them, let alone invite them out. Oddly enough, none of the women whom I had once thought attractive had come; they were either dead or lived out of state. But I may have failed to recognize the women who were present because their appearance had changed so. A classmate who shall remain anonymous told me later that when he was in high school he thought the women in our class were singularly ugly, "real dogs," but now he found them better looking. Certainly the war years were not a time when adolescent girls looked their best. The poverty of the Great Depression and wartime shortages conspired to limit women to cheap and unattractive clothing, and cosmetics were not universally approved of or used. The women of the class of '43 were certainly better dressed and made up in 1993. That the difference in appearance was a product of the times and not the genes seemed confirmed when Ruth Hunter Roberts, who was distantly related and who was not considered one of the better-looking girls in the high school class, proudly showed me a picture of her daughter who was strikingly beautiful and had once won the title of Miss Iowa.

As for myself not being recognized, it was understandable. I was sixteen and small when I graduated from high school, almost invisible. In my senior year I was in the class play and had finally been noticed. As a result, my yearbook entry read "just an actor at heart," a mischaracterization of my high school career. My main activity had been FFA, of which I was president in my senior year. But this was beyond the pale of those who edited the high school yearbook, *Maroon Memories*, as the farm boys' organization was not fashionable.

Oskaloosa had changed its appearance somewhat in my absence, but its population remained between ten thousand and eleven thousand. The town square still was the center of Oskaloosa, dominated by the three-story brick courthouse built in 1886 and containing a small, tree-lined park with an art nouveau bandstand built in 1912. (Iowa towns have many such bandstands, built with tax money and designed to bring music to the populace before the days of radio.) Also in the park was the only public nod to the town's Indian heritage, a statue of Chief Mahaska with an appropriate inscription. Yet the stereotypical small-town square now had more of an air of a stage setting than a real business center. The two-story brick buildings surrounding the park no longer housed the commercial heart of the town I remembered—clothing stores, movie houses, shoe stores, bookstores, restaurants, and drugstores. The ground floors now held antique shops, gift shops, law offices, and various obviously lower-rent businesses. The main shopping district had shifted to the west, to a downtown mall that had its entrance on the square next to a former bank and movie theater. The one remaining restaurant on the square, the Chief Mahaska, had achieved a measure of fame with its inclusion in Jane and Michael Stern's *Road Food Good Food*. I went to the café and found the food familiar but no longer the kind I could eat. It was the food of my youth about which the Sterns rhapsodized:

> Next to the salad bar are the day's pies. The one that cried out to be tasted was rhubarb, tightly packed into a lard crust. This was pie mastery, as subtle as the pasta salad was loud, the tart flavor of the rhubarb deftly sugared but not overwhelmed.

> Back at the table, as we plunged through salads, the pork tenderloin arrived. Wow! It was a mammoth meal, the cutlets overwhelming a large plate. Sandy-crusted, nearly greaseless, with a thick center of meat in proportion to the breading, it was classy pork loin, for plates instead of sandwiches.

> As we polished it off, and surveyed the emptied plates on the table, it occurred to us that the meal—broad pork tenderloin, pull-all-stops salad bar, and wizardly rhubarb pie— was a veritable definition of heartland café cookery.

The only evidence of ethnic diversity in the town's business district were three Chinese restaurants—two more than in my youth—but one of them was closed. There were no African Americans, or Asians for that matter, on the streets or in the stores that Saturday morning.

After viewing the sights of Oskaloosa, I headed south to see recent areas of industrial growth near Eddyville, a small hamlet on the Des Moines River, about twelve miles away. The road was familiar; I had ridden on it many times with my grandfather, who went to the Eddyville Sales Barn on

Thursdays for the livestock auctions. The road passed the acreage my uncle Carl had purchased when he retired from active farming as well as mounds of spoil from long-abandoned coal mines, reminders of the area's past prosperity.

Mahaska County's first boom had occurred in the decades after the Civil War with the discovery of rich seams of coal underlying the equally rich soil of glaciated Iowa. For thirty years the county produced more coal than any other county in the state; in some years production amounted to more than half the state total. The mines had a profound impact upon the region. They created a small affluent group that had large homes in Oskaloosa and whose descendants formed what upper class the town contained. The mines also attracted a highly diverse ethnic population of workers. The first laborers to arrive were of English, Welsh, Scottish, Italian, and Swedish extraction, who came in such numbers that the county population in 1880 was 35,000, a figure outnumbering that of the present day. Among those who came were the Lewis family of Welsh origin, whose first son was born in Beacon, a suburb of Oskaloosa, but whose more famous son, John L., was born in Lucas in a neighboring county.

Mining became an important enterprise in Iowa; my relatives had worked in the industry. One, C. A. Hoover, began the Iowa Coal Washing Company in 1911, and my father, as a young man, hauled coal in a horse-drawn wagon from a mine on my uncle's farm as a supplement to the family's main business of farming.

Labor trouble soon plagued the mines. In 1880 the first wave of miners struck at the Muchakinock's Coal Camp of the Oskaloosa Consolidated Coal Company, located halfway between Oskaloosa and Eddyville. The company responded by bringing in African-American strikebreakers from Virginia to replace recalcitrant workers. The camp lasted only

another twenty years as the coal proved to be of low quality—soft, with a high rock and sulfur content—and the
seams played out. Consolidated thereupon closed the mine
in 1900 to seek better prospects elsewhere. Many of the
African-American miners moved to the town of Buxton in
neighboring Monroe County, making it one of the very few
black towns in Iowa.

Few of the once numerous African-American families in
the county were left when I was growing up, probably because there was little industry to sustain them. We had only
one black in my senior class; his name appears in *Maroon
Memories* but not his senior picture. His description is of "a
gentleman from sole to crown," and his predicted future in
1960 was as a dancer: "Elmer Hobbs has just signed a life
term contract with Metro Golden [sic] Mayer Studio, replacing Bill Robinson." But his name does not even appear in
"Fifty Years of Memories," the list of graduates and their en-
capsulated life stories that was distributed to returning
alumni. Like the black miners of Muchakinock Camp, he has
faded from sight.

The town of Eddyville had changed little since I had last
seen it. The sales barn where I was scolded for accidentally
kicking chaff down an old farmer's neck was either gone or
diverted to other use, but the town was still basically a one-
street hamlet. Outside the tiny business district, however,
were two major agri-industries. Cargill had built a large
grain-processing plant there in 1985, taking advantage of the
ample supply of corn grown in the area and the readily available water from the Des Moines River to make corn syrup, a
major sweetener for soft drinks that had become a stiff com-
petitor to sugar in recent years. In 1986 Ajinamoto, a Japanese company, had located next to Cargill to utilize its corn
by-products to derive lysine, an amino acid used in animal
feed. Until 1991, when Archer Daniels Midland entered the

business, Ajinamoto shared the American market with another Japanese firm, Kyowa Hakka, and a Korean company, Sewon.

This infusion of capital from Minnesota and Japan had had little impact on the physical appearance of Eddyville. Nor did there appear to be a large influx of Japanese in the town; the workers were drawn from neighboring farms and hamlets. The two processors had added four hundred new jobs to the area and revitalized a rail link between Oskaloosa, a railway hub, and Eddyville by filling ten trains a day with corn going to the plant and the same number with products being hauled away. The agri-business presence had altered the complexion of the county by connecting it more firmly to the larger world in a way that could not have been dreamed of in the wartime days of the Class of '43.

The corn-processing plants had wrought changes in the markets available to area farmers. When I was growing up, we never sold corn but bought a little when we had fed the animals all of ours. One neighbor, John Edgren, sold some of his corn every year by simply tacking a hand-lettered sign on a post saying "Corn for Sale." Itinerant truckers, many from Missouri, would stop to fill their trucks that had hauled hickory or other fence posts north. There was no major international market in the area that would buy corn; now, thanks to a global marketplace, there was.

I returned to the Inn for lunch, but the organizers of the reunion had left the afternoon free. I took advantage of the opportunity to visit my parents' graves in Bloomfield Cemetery. En route I drove by my father's farm, which he had been forced to sell in 1952 because of ill health. I had always fantasized that I would return to live on that farm for, as memories of the hard farm life faded, one pleasant remembrance persisted. Before the farm was electrified in 1937, the nights, especially during the coldest part of winter, were crisp and black, with only brilliant starlight disrupting the total dark. I had missed that blackness, for, as David E. Nye has said in his marvelously informative book, *Electrifying America*, few if any of us know what genuine darkness is any more. Even isolated farms now have all-night lights burning on barnyard poles.

I found the farm for sale. The prospects for total darkness, however, had vanished, for Musco, a company in Oskaloosa that specialized in providing floodlights for night activities, had bought a thirteen-acre field opposite our farmhouse to use as an experimental site for its products. The field was as bright as the one in *Field of Dreams*, which, incidentally, Musco had illuminated. My dreams of returning to the farm had vanished with the dark; my "Field of Dreams" had gone with the appearance of the movie.

From the farm I drove the two miles to the site of the Bloomfield School, which had been situated on the crossroads opposite the Bloomfield Friends Church—miles I had walked for eight years. The road retained the crushed rock I remembered after the mud road had been improved, and gave off a powdery white dust that soon covered the rental car and drifted into adjoining fields. While the road was familiar, many landmarks had disappeared. Most of the fences dividing farms into neat rectangles were gone; so too were the pastures where cows and horses usually fed; the animals were gone as well. These were no longer general-purpose but grain-producing farms, so there was no need for fences, pastures, or animals. There was no need for people, either: of the seven farmhouses on the route, only two remained. Where were the families who had lived there? Some of the older members lay in the cemetery; the younger ones had gone on to greener fields or to city streets.

Neither Bloomfield School nor Bloomfield Friends Church still stands on the top of the hill where day lilies and wild roses now grow in the grader ditches. Rural consolidation in the late 1940s closed the school. The neighboring farmer, Joe Gray, who had married Miss Anderson, stored grain in the building for a time before it was demolished. Now a TV repeater tower marks the spot. It too will probably vanish soon, leaving no trace of human habitation. Gone too was the white frame church. But a lacy iron archway over the dirt road leading into the cemetery identified the graveyard. There many of my relatives are buried.

As I drove back to town by a different route, passing my grandfather's and uncle's farms, one of which adjoined the cemetery and had long since passed into other hands, I experienced a profound sense of rootlessness. The physical layout of these farms had reflected, in a tangible way, the emotional structure of my extended family, of which my grandfather was the linchpin.

Before the evening banquet, the highlight of the weekend, I had wanted to visit an old friend's house. I went by Bob Bernstein's home, but he wasn't there. I had met Bob and become close friends with him when we sold wool and scrap iron to his father's company. The Jews in Oskaloosa have become almost as invisible as African Americans. In 1900 there were thirty-five Jewish families in the town; by 1916 they had built a synagogue. As was the case in many other small Midwestern towns, Jews were in the retail clothing business, or, like the Bernsteins, hides, wool, and scrap metals. In the 1930s their stores were still prosperous. By the 1940s, however, the competition from chain stores such as Sears, Montgomery Ward, and JCPenney, and the movement of Jewish children into professional or business life in larger cities elsewhere, reduced the number of families and forced the synagogue to close. By the 1950s the families of Bernstein and his uncle, who built and renovated houses, were about the only ones left.

Bob's brothers had looked for greater opportunities in places such as Chicago and Jacksonville, leaving him, as the youngest, to care for his aging parents and eventually to run the business. This presented Bob with several difficult personal problems. A sophisticated, gregarious, and well-educated fellow, he met few people with whom he could talk seriously and no women he could hope to marry who would pass muster with his parents. He went on arranged dates in Des Moines and Chicago, but the distances and circumstances involved were not conducive to making or sustaining an intimate relationship.

It was at this juncture that I failed Bob, a failure that still haunts me. He had fallen in love with a Lebanese woman, a Christian, who taught music at Penn College, the local school in Oskaloosa. She reciprocated and agreed to convert, but his parents strenuously opposed the match. Bob then secretly planned to elope to Chicago, saying that he and I were going for a weekend visit—but he neglected to tell me. His mother, suspicious of his story, phoned me and asked if I was going. Startled, I said no, whereupon she became ill and told Bob she would die if he left. He stayed. Eventually, after his parents died, he married a widow with children, and as he became older he spent more and more time in California where he found a Jewish community he had not been part of earlier in life.

The class banquet that night was at the country club; each of us wore a photocopy of our high school senior picture, thoughtfully provided by the reunion organizers. These were a big help to me and to others, for no one recognized me still. Two classmates, Harold Burdick and Lee Knox (both former FFA members), amused themselves by covering my badge and asking others who I was. Few knew. Truth to tell, I had not recognized either of them. Harold Burdick had coached for a time in a number of schools but was now a night auditor at a hotel in Independence, Missouri. I had played basketball with Lee on FFA teams in high school. Like Harold, he had once been thin but now was much heavier. He had never left Oskaloosa; he had worked construction all his life. Both men had never been farmers but had been typical of those who took vocational agricultural classes.

None of the returnees appeared to be spectacularly successful—and, of course, the most unsuccessful probably had not come (some who lived in Oskaloosa never appeared). One prosperous-looking person was Bob Lynn, who acted as our master of ceremonies. He was still slim and young-looking, as was his wife. Bob's family had a poultry hatchery at the edge of town, and he and his first wife, Martha, had later opened a restaurant. He had sold the hatchery to Con Agra, a major agri-business firm, and had continued in the same location as general manager of the poultry sales branch and refrigerated trucking company. He represented a trend that I had not seen when growing up, the replacement of small businesses serving local farmers with corporate giants.

Unlike Bob Bernstein, many of my classmates had wed women who were native to the area. Most had moved from the farm to the city. Vernon Wells, a farm-born boy like me and one of the class successes, gave me his copy of the 1939 eighth-grade graduation program from Mahaska County rural schools. The 160-plus rural graduates, many of whom began high school, made up an important segment of the Class of 1943. Yet there were only two people at the dinner who were retired farmers. A few farmers' widows attended, but the intent of my youthful peers to return to the farm had been frustrated by changes in the larger society. They had moved on, as I had, to other work and other lives.

Wells's career provides an excellent mini-history of those changes. After naval service, Wells began a construction business by using accumulated pay and first digging basements with a backhoe, just in time to prosper from the postwar building boom. He expanded into farming and actually bought a number of the farms lining the road where I had walked to school. It had been his ambition, he told me, to own all the farms along that one-mile stretch of road, but he had later sold his properties except for one small plot he used for equipment storage. With the proceeds he built several large apartment buildings which he rented to low-income individuals, most of them elderly women, who were eligible for federal rent subsidies. My cousin's ex-wife, who managed the buildings, called Wells an ideal landlord who replaced old appliances before they became a problem and who insisted on high standards of maintenance. It was his large house I had seen earlier in the country; he lived there in the summer but spent his winters in Tucson where he owned a commercial building. One of the most successful members of the class, Wells had anticipated economic changes better than most, benefiting from federal investment in postwar GI benefits and FHA housing, farm subsidies, and low-income housing assistance.

The impact of World War II and the subsequent national security state had shaped the working lives of other former farm boys. Eugene Hensyel, a classmate of Wells's in Fairview School in Harrison Township, had worked in the atomic energy industry in Washington State all his life. Bill Hickman, from Evans School in Garfield Township, had joined the navy and flown lighter-than-air-craft on submarine patrols in World War II. He remained in the service until he retired in Florida.

Two other classmates, one present at the reunion and the other not, had gone from the farm to the church. They were Sydney Rooy and Clarence E. Van Heukeleom, both Dutch.

The Dutch were newcomers in the eyes of earlier pioneers. According to Jacob Van Der Zee's *The Hollanders of Iowa*, the Dutch had originally settled in Pella, a town located north and west of Oskaloosa in an adjoining county. After the Civil War, Dutch farmers moved south and east into Mahaska County. By 1870 the Dutch population was 318; by 1895 it had risen to 523. The next decade was one of great increase, swelling the Dutch presence to three-fourths of the population in Black Oak Township and one-third in Richland Township in the northern part of the county. The first Christian Reformed Church moved to Oskaloosa in 1903 from Leighton in the northeast corner of the county, signaling the continuing Dutch migration to the south.

Both Sydney Rooy and his brother Martin John went to Oskaloosa High School, but their paths then diverged. Martin John, the oldest, became a tenant farmer before being forced to end his working days because of multiple sclerosis. Moving to Grand Rapids, Michigan, where Sydney had gone to Calvin College, Martin John opened a small card shop before dying relatively young. Sydney eventually became a Christian Reformed minister in Argentina. He had not returned for the fifty-year reunion, but several class members reported, with great awe, that he had appeared a year earlier, home on furlough from Buenos Aires, wearing a large cowboy hat. I found it difficult to picture Sydney in hedonistic Buenos Aires preaching to ex-patriot Dutch residents. He had successfully negotiated a great cultural change.

Clarence Van Heukeleom had not traveled as far and was at the reunion. He wanted to reminisce about our high school days and about Ted Collins, who had taught vocational agriculture classes. Like Martin John, Clarence had farmed after graduation from high school but after a time had become convinced that he was called to preach. He became an ordained Christian Reformed minister and preached in churches in Colorado, Minnesota, California, and Iowa, in addition to having been a missionary, like Sydney, but to the Mescalero Apaches in the Southwest. He had seen more of the world than most members of the class, having visited Russia, England, Holland, Germany, Austria, Mexico, and Canada. Yet the list of hobbies he pursued in his retirement in Orange City, Iowa (a Dutch enclave), seemed still quite rustic. These included "toy trains; two horses; buggies; sleigh; parade work with cart before the horse (horse pushed the cart)." Had Clarence really left the farm and the Dutch community he had known in his youth?

On Sunday I was inducted, along with other class members, into the fifty-plus year club of graduates of Oskaloosa High School. I sat next to Kathryn Verbeek (Veldhuizen) who was the Class of '43 co-valedictorian and was also Dutch. Isabel Sarvis, the other co-valedictorian, had not attended.

Kathryn was less prominent in high school—I don't remember her at all from those days because she was so quiet and unobtrusive. Her life had been entirely rural: she had stayed in the area, had married a farmer who died in 1979, and had then remarried another. She had taught school for a time but was retired with her husband to a house run as a bed-and-breakfast near the country club.

Among those at the luncheon was my sixth-grade teacher, Maxine Anderson, a third-generation American of Swedish ancestry, who was only ten years older than I. As noted, she had married Joe Gray, whose farm had adjoined the school and whose family were longtime residents in the area. After retiring from the farm, she had moved her antique shop, The Henhouse, from the farm to the town square.

As I drove back to Des Moines that afternoon, I tried to make sense of the weekend gathering. I was struck by the fact that, as far as I could recall, no one had spoken of money or possessions. Most of my classmates were retired; most had been middle class or even working class. The entries in the "Fifty Years of Memories" had not boasted of success, except in terms of numbers of children or grandchildren. Greed seemed to have gone away with our youth. Perhaps we were too tired to struggle any more for things, or perhaps we were wiser. Perhaps we enjoyed an affluence we could only have dreamed about in the still poverty-stricken times of the early forties.

In high school I had never really felt a part of the group, a loner not by choice but by circumstance. Now, oddly enough, I felt more connected. Was it because we were all survivors, or was it because we were more understanding of how little our own efforts had shaped our lives? Conversely I found it interesting that two members of a very closed, tightly knit community—the Christian Reformed church— chose some way of individuating themselves: Sydney with his cowboy hat and Clarence with his cart before the horse. That individualism—if in truth it was an effort to stand out from the crowd—now seemed almost as foreign to me as the orange-robed Buddhist monks I saw begging on the Shijo bridge in Kyoto.

At the same time the community was far more a part of the larger world than it had ever been. The newspaper read by residents was not locally owned. It belonged to a woman, Roseanne Barr, and her husband of the time, who had achieved fame as a comedian in that den of iniquity, Hollywood. Part of the area's prosperity flows from Japanese investors, from a once-hated enemy. The corn raised by local farmers is no longer processed at J. H. Wake, a feed mill, for local animal consumption. The decisions affecting the community's economic future are now often made elsewhere, in boardrooms in Minnesota or Tokyo.

Finally, on a personal level, I had become more aware of the world I lost. Now it served as a reminder of the past. At the Nelson Pioneer Farm, a historically preserved acreage where historical society members have been collecting old buildings and artifacts, I found the Spring Creek Township Voting House, supposedly the first structure west of the Mississippi specifically devoted to elections, a place not unfamiliar to me, and the post office at Wright, a crossroads hamlet where I had mailed in my first draft registration after being notarized by the part-time clerk. Both are now only memories.

The Indians have gone from the area, leaving little trace of their presence. My family, the Hoovers, are gone too, with only gravestones marking their hundred-year residence. The farm life I knew was gone, and so were those who badly wanted to be farmers. They are history, and so, I think, is the Iowa boy.

Index

A NOTE ON THE AUTHOR

Dwight W. Hoover was born in Oskaloosa, Iowa, in 1926 and grew up on a farm near there. He studied at a local college and then received a Ph.D. in history from the University of Iowa. He taught at Bethune-Cookman, Kansas State University, and Ball State University, where he was also director of the Center for Middletown Studies. He has twice been a Fulbright professor in Hungary. Mr. Hoover's other books include *Magic Middletown*, *A Pictorial History of Indiana*, *The Red and the Black*, and *A Teacher's Guide to American Urban History*. He is now "semi-retired" and lives with his wife Jan in Sarasota, Florida.